A MULTICULTURED LIFE

A MULTICULTURED LIFE

From the Little Red School House to Halls of Academe
and Corporate Board Rooms

DOLORES WHARTON

Doeclif Publishing
Cooperstown, NY

Printed and bound by Thomson-Shore, Inc.

The paper in this book meets the guidelines for
permanence and durability of the Committee on
Production Guidelines for Book Longevity of the
Council on Library Resources.

Library of Congress Control Number: 2018955095

ISBN 978-0-692-03512-2

CONTENTS

A MULTICULTURED LIFE

CHAPTER 1

"And Whose Little Girl Are You?"

How brisk, bold, and magical the world seemed to a little girl growing up in New York City in the 1920s and 1930s. Even as the Great Depression cast its long shadow, a joyful symphony of Manhattan's vibrant rhythms perpetually filled the air. Duke Ellington turned out hits like "Sophisticated Ladies" and "Take The A Train." The brand new Empire State Building gave us the tallest building in the world, and the George Washington Bridge gave us the longest span, capturing the imaginations of adults across town. However, my first vivid memory from childhood is of a wedding reception that I attended in my mother's hometown of Philadelphia. Even today, more than nine decades distant, I need only close my eyes and conjure the aroma of perfumed ladies, and the day comes rushing back to life:

As my mother and I enter the crowded room, I, a precocious and no doubt spoiled five-year-old, pull away from her side and slip through the press of people, allured by the ornately decorated rooms of the bride's family home. There are no Caucasians present, though it would be difficult to distinguish them from many of those mingling in the mix of multi-hued wedding guests. Without exception, the guests are dressed fashionably, with stylish attire and stunning jewelry. The men are doctors, lawyers, and undertakers; the women are school teachers and social workers; one or two are caterers. Indeed, one matron, whose husband's firm is catering the event, lends a watchful eye as her waitstaff make their way through the crowd, bearing silver trays laden with chicken and crab croquettes, creamed sweetbreads on toast points, and slices of Virginia ham rolled with watercress—to accompany the Champagne punch served in crystal cups. Such is the life of many accomplished upper-middle-class Negroes along the Eastern Seaboard in the 1920s and 1930s.

Believing myself unnoticed as I wander about, I am surprised when a most elegant lady steps in front of me and bows to my height.

"And whose little girl are you?"

I promptly respond, "My mother is Josephine Bradford Duncan"

"Oh, you are a Bradford!" my inquisitor exclaims, wrapping her arms around me. Your mother and I were schoolmates many, many years ago. Take me to your mom immediately."

Although excited at being an out-of-town guest at this largely adult gathering, I am at ease in grasping my new friend's hand, leading her to my mother, who is standing among a circle of old chums. My self-assurance comes naturally as I watch my beautiful mother being blithely regaled by women she has known since childhood. Their conversation is laughter-filled as they demand details of her life in cosmopolitan New York, where she has lived since marrying my father, co-owner of a prominent funeral home in Harlem. Her friends want to hear everything about the glamorous "Joe"—their name for my mom—whom they know as vivacious, coquettish, and clever, though not presumed to make a willful stand among the power-driven women of Harlem. My mother clearly loves being back in the fold of old Philadelphia society. She beams as I approach, announcing to her friends, "Enough about me. I want you to meet my daughter, Dolores."

You, my reader, might say, "Dolores, you fantasize! Or, if not that, your story of Black affluence matters little when considering majority of Blacks, past and present, in American history."

"Hold on!" I insist.

My memoir begins in an age when cultural values were respected throughout society which included pockets of prosperous Blacks in Eastern seaboard cities. I offer my childhood vignette as background to a complex life that is representative of a larger number of people of color—historically—than you might have otherwise imagined. Above all, mine is the story of an American Black woman whose life has been enriched by a series of unexpected adventures. My first twelve years were spent in Harlem with my mother, father, and older brother, while being formally educated at a primarily white private school in Greenwich Village. There, we were exposed to Eastern and Western cultures, learning enhanced by frequent trips to New York City's many museums, whose magnificent collections left an indelible imprint on me.

My world changed dramatically during my teen years, when we relocated to a clannish New England town where some in the community were unaccepting because of my race. Though bigotry with all its venom was widely discussed during my younger New York City years, I was not subjected to any of its malicious iterations before arriving in the old Yankee towns of Connecticut—though, even then, the offenses were subtle.

My marriage to a man of intelligence, grace, and authority made my life literally otherworldly. I lived in and savored the cultures of Southeast Asia, observing the region's varied traditions, learning to converse in the Malay language and to interact with people from around the world, particularly Malays, local and foreign-born Chinese, and South Indians. My universe was further seasoned and expanded by the differences I encountered in the various diplomatic embassies where we were frequently entertained. As the fine arts became my life's trajectory, I embraced the young Malaysian artists who were building their nation's newly burgeoning art scene. My patronage eventually led me to both participate in and help record the history of this exciting development.

Holding firm and embracing our two adored sons, my husband and I redirected our course in different ways, each time steering cautiously but confidently over unmarked paths. These varying experiences were major influences shaping my individuality as First Lady of two American institutions of higher education. They also provided me the opportunity to serve as outside director of several multinational corporations. Big Business in the United States had been almost exclusively a white-male domain. But in the 1960s, Blacks and women began demanding inclusion, which pushed some courts and enlightened corporate leaders to respond affirmatively to calls for recognition. I was privileged to be among the few chosen to stand in the vanguard of a dynamic change in corporate American history.

Race has always imposed a definitive mark on my identity. Intentionally or unintentionally, there exists a perception that every person of African descent is less intelligent compared with those of white origins. Being perceived as inherently, if not genetically, stupid and incompetent, all people of color, even to the most minimal degree, bear the burden of race hatred. Thus, there are millions of Black people who are afflicted with the hurtful effects of institutional prejudice.

By the grace of many gods, there are some of us who have not had to face the more extreme, life-demeaning confrontations resulting from discrimination. Though always conscious of racist atrocities, I have been protected against most offenses by my parents, my husband, and a host of intelligent individuals with whom I have had the good fortune to interact.

And so I came to recognize my responsibility to make a contribution toward the struggle against the effects of race hatred. As part of my engagement in corporate board oversight, I asked myself, "What are the drawbacks facing young Blacks and women in the corporations I serve, and how might I influence their upward mobility?" I responded to that challenge by proposing the creation of social responsibility committees, which were established within the corporate structure of the companies I served as a director. Such committees had the clout to review and improve the quality of life for workers and their families, as well as for the local community and society at large.

From my sky-box as a corporate director, I had a unique vantage point from which I could explore ways to address issues of upward mobility, primarily for people of color, particularly women. It was with considerable gratification that these efforts led me to create the Fund for Corporate Initiatives (FCI). Through this foundation I influenced some two hundred talented young leaders of tomorrow. I created FCI with my husband's strong encouragement, and under its umbrella, I administered three distinct programs that for twenty-one years were funded primarily with my corporate fees. My mission was to mentor young minority men and women, preparing them to walk into the executive suites of corporate America, where power resides, as sophisticated young professionals.

This story reflects four factors that are uncharacteristic of those who have experienced the atrocities of racism: I was shielded in my early years by the accomplishments of my forebears reaching back to the mid-1800s, who had acquired social and economic standing in the Black community. My exposure to multiple cultures and love of the arts offered a broad universal perspective. I shared my journey with a husband of exceptional achievement, and we boldly risked taking several complementary paths.

Today, the most popular stories of American Blacks emphasize poverty, violence, and social separation. While I strongly endorse—even applaud—these essential writings that expose Black adversity, it also is important to provide a more complete understanding about the complex and multilayered Black experience. Despite the terror-filled history of slavery and racial discrimination, there also have evolved significant cohorts of successful Blacks in the greater society.

Overcoming seemingly impossible obstacles, Black people have made extraordinary contributions to the development of this country. The accounting of the path-breakers who have contributed to the formidable history of Blacks is found in every generation. Each has built further upon what our ancestors have bequeathed. My story begins with reflections upon my own family members who participated in the greater society as activist citizens.

As I begin to recount a lifetime of experiences, I realize how deeply I have been shaped by those early years in the exhilarating energy of New York City and in the cultural embrace of my family.

CHAPTER 2

Harlem, Greenwich Village, and Beyond

When my mother was barely a year old, the family expanded suddenly with the arrival of twin sisters. To ease the child-care responsibilities thrust on her parents, she was taken in and raised by her grandparents, James T. and Josephine Wells Bradford. Thus, my mom, who was named for her grandmother, came to lead a privileged life as the only young child in the household of prosperous grandparents. They called her Joseph.

James T. Bradford owned a greengrocery in greater Washington, D.C. As a young man, my great-grandfather had worked for the white proprietor, selling fruits and vegetables in an open market. Nickel by nickel, he saved enough to eventually purchase the business, which soon included a major catering service that was well-patronized by wealthy white clients. Before long the shop was replicated in Baltimore, where it also thrived. Over the years, James T. acquired a large family home in Philadelphia, an oceanside vacation home in Sea Isle, Maryland, and several investment houses in Philadelphia. He even partnered heavily in a Black-owned bank. The patriarch was generous to his wife, their six children, and his various grandchildren, nieces, and nephews. He lived well—as did many of his friends—enjoying fine home furnishings and table settings of silver, china, and crystal, some of which survive in my home today.

The household employed several servants, according to the 1900 U.S. Census, including Mary Gaskins, forty-five, and George Washington, fifty. However, my mother only spoke of culinary help when recounting her grandfather's admonition that "Ladies do not go into the kitchen"—advice I have enthusiastically taken to heart.

James T. Bradford,
my maternal great-grandfather
(b. 1842, d. 1913)

James T. Bradford's obituary,
*Baltimore African-American
News* (February 15, 1913)

Josephine Wells Bradford, my maternal great-grandmother
(b. 1844, d. after 1920)

May and Blanche Bradford, daughters
of James T. and Josephine

James T. drank a toddy or two before the evening meal. He regularly attended the Episcopal Church in his morning frock coat, tipping his hat to the ladies. But most significant was that a Black man in the 1880s was successful in business, was respected in the greater community, and lived a comfortable and responsible life.

My mother idolized her grandfather, but when she spoke of her grandmother, her voice would soften into reverent tones. "Gramma was an angel, a real live angel," she'd say. "Every day she would sit at the living room window reading her Bible and waving to neighbors who walked past."

Josephine Bradford's mother—my grandmother—had a personality that dramatically contrasted with the very sedate Bradfords. Eliza Johnson Bradford said whatever came to mind—her comments more humorous than hurtful. She enjoyed betting at the racetrack and playing backgammon late into the night. She was known to make fun of herself and in jest would exclaim, "Eliza Johnson! A name fit for a mule!" But she didn't look like barnyard stock. In fact, she modeled hats professionally for an aunt who was a milliner. Although Eliza was unpredictable in social settings, the very conservative Bradfords tended to forgive her antics, accepting her as a good woman willing to contribute more than her share to the support of her family, especially as her husband was not the provider his own father had been.

Mom was twenty-four when she married V. Kenneth Duncan in September 1923. Aunt May, James T.'s spinster daughter, who still lived at home and helped raise my mother, sensed potential problems for the marriage and offered my mother a trip to Europe if she would delay the wedding indefinitely. But Mom was smitten. Kenneth Duncan's urbane grace was far greater than that of the other beaus who had called upon her. Marriage to Kenneth Duncan was, simply, destiny. He was the very image of what she wanted in a husband: well spoken, debonair, bearing the self-confidence of a successful businessman.

My father came from a family of three sons (John Jr., Kenneth, and Willie Henry, known as Sonny) and two daughters (Rosebud and Alma Zola). My paternal grandfather, John Duncan Sr., was the proprietor of a taxi livery service in Greenville, South Carolina. After his death, my grandmother, Cora, moved the family to New York City. In 1920 John Jr., whom I knew as Uncle Jack, established the Duncan Brothers Funeral Home in Harlem, with my father as full partner and their mother, Cora, as a *very* controlling investor. The business flourished until 1934, when Uncle Jack died.

Ancestors are never chosen, but it was my good fortune to have achievers across the generations from both sides of the family. They were entrepreneurs; some also were politicians. Hiram W. Duncan served as a radical member of the South Carolina State General Assembly and then Senate during Reconstruction in the 1870s and 1880s. James T. Bradford attended the Republican National Convention in 1900 and led a committee that visited Theodore Roosevelt when he was nominated as vice president.

A year after my parents' marriage, my brother John W. Duncan III was born. Named for his uncle, little Jackie was expected to be a chip off the old Duncan block. I was born Dolores Mae Duncan three years later, during a time my mother remembered as the happiest of her first marriage.

Cora May Duncan, my paternal grandmother (b. 1870, d. 1950)

John W. "Uncle Jack" Duncan Jr.,
my father's older brother (b. 1891, d. 1933)

Kenneth Duncan, my father (b. 1899, d. 1952)

Hiram W. Duncan, 1868, fourth row, second from left, a radical member of the
South Carolina State Legislature. Hiram was my paternal great-great-great uncle.

John W. Duncan III,
my brother, in his U.S. Army
uniform during WWII
(b. Aug 4, 1924, d. Oct 15, 1982)

Josephine Wells
Bradford Duncan Owens,
my mother (b. April 16, 1899,
d. April 27, 1986)

HARLEM LIFE

Harlem was a brilliant reflection of the City, but recast in sepia tones. The Harlem Renaissance flourished with intellectual and creative talent—artists, musicians, photographers, and especially literary lights, among them Langston Hughes, Zora Neale Hurston, Countee Cullen, and James Weldon Johnson. The jazz and racy nightclubs and Prohibition-era speakeasies were separate scenes from my own life. I was simply too young and otherwise engaged in the business of growing up to be exposed to the high-flying fast life of Harlem.

Indeed Harlem in the late 1920s and early 1930s was culturally and commercially vibrant. Seventh Avenue was one of Harlem's main boulevards, and much of city life seemed to converge at our intersection of 135th Street: clanging trolley bells, honking horns from high-roofed automobiles with wide running boards, massive double-decker buses, a smattering of horse-drawn delivery wagons. The community teemed with a fascinating mix of people—Black, white, and varying shades of brown, well-dressed, unkempt, wealthy, derelict—all hurrying about their business.

This urban microcosm was the result of the second wave of Black migration to the North, the first having taken place in the 1880s and 1890s. In fact, Blacks had lived in Harlem since the 1630s, though in very small numbers, which slowly grew into tens of thousands by the start of the twentieth century. A real estate crash in 1904 led to a mass influx of a Black population that eventually outnumbered the previously dominant Jewish and Italian families. But while Jews and Italians could assimilate in other neighborhoods, Blacks found themselves for the most part isolated and virtually trapped in Harlem.

While this created great challenges and inequities, it also provided an energy unequaled anywhere else in the city. Right in the middle of this bustling metropolis, at 2303 Seventh Avenue, stood the Duncan building, a four-story, family-owned property. At the street level was the Duncan Brothers Funeral Home, which included a reception area, a chapel with organ, and offices; the basement served as the embalming lab. The second floor, with separate, private entry, was commercial space leased to dentists. One longtime tenant was Dr. Hap Delany, whose sisters, Sarah and Elizabeth, would years later become the centenarian authors of *Having Our Say: The Delany Sisters' First 100 Years*, a 1993 best seller that was made into a Broadway play. Outside the second-floor office space was a secured door that led to two residential apartments above. My grandmother, Cora, lived on the third floor, and my dad, mom, Jackie, and I lived above her.

One Christmas, when the second-floor commercial space was vacant, Mom turned it into a fantasy land of toys for Jackie and me—a dollhouse, soft and clay dolls, games, coloring books, wooden puzzles, and a tricycle for me. For Jackie, Santa dropped off the latest model mini-auto with pedals. The little vehicle was purchased when a white salesgirl at Macy's Herald Square told my eight-year-old brother, who had climbed into the car, to get out immediately, a paying customer might want to buy it. My mother, infuriated, flashed: "Well, the car is his. I am buying it for him. He can sit in it as long as he likes!"

Though Seventh Avenue was dominated by mercantile establishments, it was not unusual to find living quarters over the businesses between 125th and 155th streets—this was the case for Black and white families alike. Such terms as *inner city* or *ghetto* were not then commonly used to describe Harlem, where many genuinely fine houses were to be found. Two blocks in particular—both the east and west sides of 138th and 139th streets between Seventh and Eighth avenues—were Black-owned properties known as Strivers' Row. These residences were eventually included in national and city historical registries.

Not all of Harlem was vital or thriving. Many of the side streets showed heartbreaking signs of poverty, neglect, and painfully poor living conditions. Such areas in Harlem existed for the simple reason that most Blacks of every income group—from rich to poor—had no choice but to live in Harlem. Buildings in other parts of the city were neither rented nor sold to Black people. There was a keen awareness of the invisible fence around Harlem imposed by Manhattan's realtors. That was where Blacks would be herded and contained.

One effect of segregation was that Harlem became a "city within a city," which thrived inside its own geographic boundaries. The professional service providers in the neighborhood—doctors, dentists, undertakers, electricians, teachers, bankers, and beauticians—were all Negro. But in the late 1920s and early 1930s, white-owned businesses also were prominent. Harlem was surprisingly diverse, with Irish-, Italian-, and Jewish-owned properties being the norm for the community. There were optometry clinics, ice cream parlors, movie houses, dry cleaners, liquor stores, and restaurants. It was a place where whites had become property owners in residence—where they earned their living and sent their children to the local schools. However, socializing with the white families, as I recall, was *verboten* for Black society. (Today the area is undergoing a reverse transformation as it enters a period of prodigious gentrification, with white realtors buying up blocks of housing as city property becomes an increasingly valuable investment.)

The Duncan Brothers Funeral Home, one of New York's first Black-owned businesses to be listed by Dun & Bradstreet, commanded respect beyond fulfilling a critical professional service for the community. (White funeral establishments simply would not bury Black people.) The butcher, the baker, the candy maker, even the policeman would individually acknowledge each of our family members. In fact, I well recall Officer Lacey, a huge Black patrolman, regularly stopping traffic on the corner of Seventh at 135th and tipping his hat as he courteously ushered my mother across the thoroughfare with Jackie and me in tow.

When there were no funeral services in progress, my father would stand in the doorway of his establishment, dapper in his conservatively cut suits as he greeted passersby with a tip of the hat—a well-brushed derby or straw bowler, depending upon the season. Prominent members of the community would stop to visit: there were the Rev. Shelton Hale Bishop, pastor of St. Philip's Episcopal Church, the largest Episcopal congregation in New York City. (Father Bishop baptized my brother and me, years later our two sons, and married Clifton and me). Also stopping by to chat awhile were such Harlem potentates as Adam Clayton Powell, the flamboyant minister and later congressman; Dr. C.B. Powell, publisher of the *Amsterdam News*. "C.B." was one of the wealthiest and most influential entrepreneurs in Harlem. Together with his business partner Phillip Savory, they established Powell & Savory Liquors, The Brown Bomber Bread Company (named for boxer Joe Louis), a life-insurance company and more. Other well-knowns were the film actor and dancer Bill "Bojangles" Robinson, singer and activist Paul Robeson, and Harry T. Burleigh, composer of Negro spirituals.

Their ranks were filled with an endless parade of less-famous and less-accomplished people as well. One of the most colorful characters was an unemployed chap who regularly sauntered by the funeral home seeking odd jobs and offering pithy one-liners such as, "I'm so broke—when I walk into a restaurant I can only afford me a bellyful of smells." The Black sense of humor has sustained the American Negro throughout our history.

One afternoon I popped in to see my dad when he was meeting with a small, simply-dressed, dark-skin woman. When my father introduced us, I abruptly turned my head and, without speaking, began to walk away. My father, detecting my youthful display of class conceit, pulled me onto his knee and spanked my bottom until I wept. It was a parental discipline promptly imposed: "One speaks, and one speaks clearly and courteously, to everyone!" My father's lesson was enduring!

At its busiest, Duncan Brothers had to schedule several funerals a day, with overflowing crowds in attendance. Dad or Uncle Jack, whomever was presiding, would greet the clergyman and stay with him until the organ began in earnest and the procession entered the chapel. I recall how one frequently officiating prelate with balding head turned upward and eyes cast down would march in solemn prayer, swaying rhythmically from side to side as he reverently walked among the grieving. He was followed by four, five, or six heaven-inspired vocalists harmonizing. The organist, usually the same small, rotund lady whose tiny feet could barely reach the pedals, filled the lily-scented sanctuary with melancholy chords. The service was a perfectly staged production with every player in place and on cue. Daddy and Uncle Jack were masters of their trade. But it was their deep respect and compassion for the families of the deceased that gave Duncan Brothers Funeral Home a reputation for refined and courteous care.

On occasion I would ride in the hearse, sitting on the armrest between my father and our chauffeur, Willie, as our vehicle led the orderly procession to the cemetery. By the time the grief-stricken family and friends had reached the gravesite, they had quieted. The ladies would smile at me with eyebrows raised, heads turned sideways as I handed each mourner a flower to toss into the grave during closing prayer. On such occasions, I felt myself a valued part of the team.

JACKIE AND ME

When at home, my brother and I often amused ourselves by gazing from our living-room window onto the street four stories below. We delighted in watching the over-size ladies returning from Sunday church as they sashayed along Seventh Avenue in high heels and huge, colorfully decorated hats, bedecked in jewelry, tipping as glamorously as Lena Horne walking onstage.

One March evening in 1935, Jackie and I were huddled as usual in our window seats when we viewed firsthand what in retrospect was a race riot. We were fascinated at the sight of Black youths commandeering open-air, double-decker buses on Seventh Avenue. We could not hear exactly what they were yelling, but their cries reflected the mounting anger from the crowd that had gathered to protest a police incident that had targeted an innocent Black youngster for shoplifting. Given the possibility of some wildly tossed bricks, bottles, or other stray missiles hitting us, our mother insisted, "Come away from the window now, children."

My father was concerned that the rage would spread and the funeral home's massive plate-glass window would be targeted. Kenneth Duncan was a genteel man who rarely lost his temper, but that night he stood in the doorway of his business with a revolver tucked into his pocket. He wasn't the only concerned proprietor. The Chinese owner of the restaurant next door painted words on his plate-glass window: ME COLORED TOO! Many windows were smashed that night, but Duncan Brothers' and the neighboring restaurant window survived unbroken.

Jackie and I observed a very different scene on the evening of June 22, 1938, when Joe Louis knocked out Germany's Max Schmeling in the first round regaining his world heavyweight title. The people of Harlem danced in the streets and cheered from the tops of the double-decker buses, unrestrained in their rejoicing. This time the exuberance was not only in celebration of the Brown Bomber's victory but also a rebuttal to Hitler's horrific Aryan claims that Germans were the master race. In hindsight, those two Harlem flare-ups demonstrated for me how the animus of racism can so dramatically threaten the civility of a society.

Jackie was a typical older brother—sometimes playfully interacting with me but more often preferring to ignore the existence of his little sister. There were days when he refused to ride home from school in the same subway car. When I became overzealous in my art classes, splashing colorful paints on my clothes, he would complain, "She's filthy and looks disgusting. I don't want to be seen with her." No matter. I adored my big brother, even when he told me I was adopted and shouldn't take snacks from the refrigerator.

Our after-school activities were primarily separate, except for weekend horseback riding at a Long Island stable where our trainer, a retired Black army cavalryman, was well received. (The posh Central Park stables, barely ten minutes from Harlem, were off-limits to Black dressage riders.) My brother's time was spent with boys his own age, cavorting in various homes, playing cowboys and Indians or cops and robbers. They traveled together—often in groups of four or five—going to the movies or swimming or boxing at the Harlem YMCA.

My after-school time, on the other hand, was more precise. My mother scheduled swimming classes at the YWCA, classical ballet lessons with Amanda Kemp (Mom was concerned that I was becoming knock-kneed), clay modeling in Augusta Savage's art classes, and overnight dates with girlfriends—downtown, uptown, and in the Bronx. There were daylong shopping trips to Fifth Avenue department stores, where we always paused long enough at Kresge's or Woolworth's stores for chocolate frosties before my eroding disposition caused me to protest against the outings. Often, when the Duncan Brothers limo was not being used, Willie would drive us to visit my mother's friends in Mount Vernon or White Plains, where a few Black families had been successful in buying homes befitting their status.

On Sunday mornings we attended St. Philip's Episcopal Church, which regularly held fund-raising fashion shows in which Jackie and I participated. The all-Black congregation delighted in our little theatrics, such as stopping in the middle of the runway, where Jackie would help me out of my suit jacket, which he would drape over his arm.

Mother had Jackie wear short pants before age ten, then knickers until he was thirteen. When not shopping for me at Best & Co., she used a dressmaker, Mrs. Burton, on 135th Street, who was known to complain, "Mrs. Duncan, I have clients other than Dolores I must sew for!" My outfits consisted of hand-tucked dresses cut well above the knee and black velvet coats made dressier with white kid gloves and black patent leather shoes.

Were these little cultural esthetics reflective of Harlem life? Of course not! But they did typify a segment of the community that included an upscale mix. Harlem was a well-rounded society that contained elements of a fully developed socioeconomic structure.

THE LITTLE RED SCHOOL HOUSE

When the time came for my formal schooling, Aunt Blanche and Aunt May, daughters of James T. Bradford, let my parents know that I should not attend the neighborhood public school where Jackie had been enrolled three years earlier. There was no protest from Philadelphia over Jackie's attending public school. After all, he was a boy, and it was good for business to have the Duncan Brothers heir-apparent attend the neighborhood school. But in due course, Jackie and I were both enrolled at the Little Red School House in Greenwich Village, far away in lower Manhattan.

The Little Red, as we came to call it, was founded by Elisabeth Irwin in 1921 but opened its doors at 196 Bleecker Street in 1932. One of the nation's first progressive schools, it then consisted of a lower school and a middle school; years later, a high school was added.

During the customary Monday morning assembly, Elisabeth Irwin personally addressed the entire student body of perhaps 150 youngsters. After the vice principal set out the programs to be followed that week, we dispersed to our assigned classes for planned activities. In the lower school, we would push our chairs about, creating circles of engagement that ranged from geography studied on huge world globes, to history readings of ancient cultures, to music and dancing with scarves Isadora Duncan–style, to science discussions about our in-house plants and animals. Desks were usually banked together for those of us working in math books or writing stories following our weekly museum field trips. Desks were also good for sitting under—just to think. This was a rare pastime, as our studies inspired a lot of high-voltage activity. Quite often our primary teacher was aided by college-student assistants; we were never at a loss for attentive care.

Many hours were spent in the basement painting, woodworking, sculpting (the school had its own kiln, unusual for lower schools in the 1930s) and weaving on looms. There were two rooms in the library, one dedicated to silence and reserved primarily for more advanced, mostly older readers. The roof served as the lower school's playground and as a space for celebrating ethnic festivals that enhanced our studies. One especially innovative project was a candy store that the nine-year-olds operated to serve the entire school at break time. The class made weekly trips to candy manufacturers and distributors to select the merchandise, for which we kept proper accounting records. Operating the store was an engaging element of the math instruction program.

Manhattan was our own, huge learning laboratory. We took weekly excursions to interesting places all around town. I viewed the George Washington Bridge early in its construction, toured Wall Street, visited bakeries and chocolate factories, and spent countless hours at the Metropolitan Museum of Art, where we learned about

Greek, Roman, and other ancient cultures. Following museum talks by professional guides, we would return to the school to make up stories about the people we imagined had possessed the antiquities on display. In good weather we carried our own versions of the ancient artifacts to the roof where we, in appropriate costumes, acted out the lifestyles under study.

Jewish students predominated at the Little Red, with Italians and Irish the next largest groups. There were perhaps no more than ten Black children enrolled at any one time. I recall three other Black female classmates along with famed Jazz pianist Fats Waller's two sons, and Paul Robeson's son, who also were students for a short time. Many of the successful families of color leaned toward the more traditional private schools, enrolling their children at Ethical Culture, Fieldston, or Dalton. In each of these Manhattan schools there was an early attempt to diversify the student body. I know personally about the efforts made at the Little Red, as my mom often was asked to recommend youngsters from Harlem as candidates.

In keeping with the school's progressive doctrine, boys and girls in the lower school used the same bathrooms. Sex differences at that age were not an issue. We were a cosmopolitan people, and we judged others according to individual characteristics: mischievous, difficult, studious, shy, fun, boring, etc. Our racial backgrounds only became significant when students wanted to share family celebrations, especially where festivities were related to our studies. Our teachers would summon the class by calling out, "People!" We were taught to be inquisitive and encouraged to speak up to explain our points of view. I considered myself an "insider" engaged in a functioning society at the Little Red.

Learning by rote memory was not standard practice in the lower school. It was believed that students could best be inspired to achieve academically by exercising their natural curiosity. The courses designed to expand our work skills often were improvisational. When *Goodnight Moon* author Margaret Wise Brown was a student teacher at the Little Red, she would take several of us at a time from the classroom to a quiet cove under an open-air stairwell, where we were encouraged to make up stories. She would prod us with questions to motivate our own make-believe narratives. We called her Margaret, as informality of first names was afforded to the rank of student teacher. The empty space allowed us to move about and interact freely, expanding upon our initial ideas as we jointly engaged in tale-telling exercises. Often, this fun-based approach to authorship was followed by the next step of reproducing our performances in words on paper. Therein lay the beginning of an original storytelling exercise.

SUMMERS IN PENNSYLVANIA

Over many summers during my youngest to pre-teen years, our family vacationed at a farm in Atglen, Pennsylvania, fifty miles west of Philadelphia. There life, the pursuit of happiness, and most certainly education were in stark contrast when compared to my lifestyle in Manhattan.

When I was eight, it was discovered that I was woefully deficient in arithmetic. Ma Wood, the widowed owner and manager of the farm, bluntly announced to my mother one day: "Dolores can talk better than any other little girl her age, but she doesn't know the multiplication tables!" Consequently, I spent every morning during the month of June in a one-room schoolhouse deciphering multiplication problems. Furthermore, I found myself in a setting where students in grades one through five altogether in one room were expected to behave as good little soldiers—we were even required to raise our hands to request permission to go to the "loo." This was a far cry from the Little Red, where we just signaled with a raised hand, got up, and left the room. These students, with Pennsylvania Dutch, Amish, and Quaker backgrounds, were all rural born and bred, and white. I was more than an outsider—I was a curiosity, my race less an oddity than the novelty of having someone in the local classroom from the big city of New York.

Most difficult for me was the unexpected challenge of having to show mastery by memorizing and repeating facts. During afternoons back-at-the-farm, I recited my homework to Ma Wood's other boarding guests, who didn't seem too annoyed by my difficulties but rather encouraged my practice sessions with suggestions such as, "You're hesitating, Dolores. You need to go over those numbers again!" By the end of that spring semester the multiplication tables had become well locked in my memory bank, never to be forgotten. This was an invaluable introduction to basic fundamentals, despite the process being painfully boring. I discovered a lot that summer, academically and socially. For example, I was associating with youngsters born into this universe as racially pure as the driven snow.

Located on a steep hill nearby, but well separated from the village of Atglen, was the local Black community of Zion Hill. The hill had its own school, church, and small grocery store. The men and women of Zion Hill worked in menial jobs near the village and were rarely seen chatting with the Caucasian villagers or browsing leisurely in Atglen's general store. There also was a larger, more integrated community of Blacks about seven miles away in the neighboring town of Parkesburg.

Ma Wood was a hard-working Black woman, who personified independence and, toward the white community, stern aloofness. Often when walking the three and a half miles from the farm to the village, my mom would tease Ma Wood, saying, "Your back gets straighter and stiffer with every step you take going into the village." Her bearing suggested a determination to command respect from every person in her world—especially white people.

Ma Wood, her daughter Louise, my mother, brother, and I occasionally visited Zion Hill and the Mt. Zion African Methodist Episcopal Church to attend social events such as cake-baking competitions, quilting displays, and most especially evening services in which the preacher held forth in demonstrative prayer. There always was music—accordions, harmonicas, boys drumming with smoothly honed sticks on anything that reverberated, and beautiful gospel singing in the church. I romped happily with the children my age—and there were lots of them—running, racing, playing tag and hide-'n'-seek, and watching the older girls skip rope, especially Double Dutch, which requires the agility to prance rhythmically from side to side between two long ropes turning in opposite directions. Zion Hill was a community with a strong ethnic culture, where we were most cordially welcomed into the fold.

Looking back, I took for granted those childhood summers in Atglen. Today I recognize the exposure as an important introduction to rural Black America, with its own customs and striking contrasts to urban life in New York City.

For a number of summers at the farm, we celebrated my July 3rd birthday by inviting the children of Zion Hill to an afternoon party in Ma Wood's garden. The boys and girls set out early in the morning on the four-mile walk to our place, then they hid among the tall reeds surrounding a pond and waited until the noon hour whistle blew. From Ma Wood's porch, we would watch as a dozen of our Zion Hill friends popped out onto the dirt road, strolling at a feigned unpretentious, leisurely gait and arriving at our gate exactly on time.

My mom, Ma Wood, and even I, the birthday girl, would have spent the previous day preparing for the party. My big brother, on the other hand, would always be too busy to help—yet always eager to join in the fun once the festivities began. The menu usually included potato salad, deviled eggs, thick slices of baked ham, and a huge coconut layer cake festooned with candles. Sometimes one of Ma Wood's other houseguests would perform magic card tricks that made everyone giggle. When the afternoon was spent, there were colorful favors for everyone to take home. Most memorable about that special day was the friendship with young people from a different Black community who generously opened their world to us—and to whom we were delighted to return the compliment.

Discourse on my father's visits to Atglen was minimal, as he spent as little time as possible vacationing in Atglen or for that matter any country setting. In the early spring, Willie would drive the whole family to the farm, a long, full-day trip. Yet invariably, as soon as we arrived, a call would come for Daddy, reporting that an important and unexpected funeral demanded his immediate return to the city. That was the last we would see of him until late August, when he and Willie would return to collect us. Our dad would telephone often in reply to our colorful postcards. But, as we all knew, he was a city man through and through.

When our mother passed her driving test, we applauded with gusto, as few women in the 1930s attempted to drive. My father bought her a small car, which we named Miss Duncan. Mother's new mobility and independence, however, afforded Daddy more personal time than could be accounted for—and, alas, more time to indulge his growing fondness for alcohol.

One quiet afternoon when we had returned home, Mom was standing in the funeral parlor, looking out the big plate-glass window at Seventh Avenue. She was chatting with Clarence Curley, an adult cousin who had been hired part-time to take care of the business when the professionals were off duty, an increasingly important role following the death of Uncle Jack in 1934. She asked Clarence, "Did your Uncle Kenneth say what time he expected to return?"

"Little Miss New York" (age 4) on a working farm in Atglen, PA,
where our family vacationed every summer from 1930 to 1936

With a grim expression, he replied slowly, "Uncle Kenny is with May Hoskins. When he is not here, he is always with May Hoskins." He paused, then added, "Aunt Joe, I really thought you knew. If not, somebody ought to tell you."

A few minutes of silence passed before Mom took my hand and led me upstairs to a very solemn apartment. Years later I learned that May Hoskins owned a beauty salon in Harlem and was an attractive woman similar in appearance to my mom, though certainly not in elegance. Once we got upstairs, a dark cloud seemed to fill the apartment and my mom's usually buoyant spirit slowly suffocated under the weight of the disclosure. Much to my mother's shock, May Hoskins and my father had become fodder for hushed gossip among our social circle. They were an "item."

CHAPTER 3

Danbury: Contrasts and Contradictions

Our parents owned a small, three-bedroom bungalow in Bethel, Connecticut, sixty miles north of the city. Set upon a sloping hillside between two groves of apple trees and a swiftly moving brook, our country home slowly began to lose its magic as a haven for our little family of four. Adversities in our parents' marriage became irreversible. Mom was in despair over Daddy's advancing alcoholism and his failings as the chief executive of the Duncan business following Uncle Jack's death. But most devastating was his romance with May Hoskins. Mom initiated divorce proceedings, and we moved from 2303 Seventh Avenue to the Connecticut cottage. In that she had no experience in the job market, Mom was proving herself to be surprisingly courageous in leaving a comfortable and secure lifestyle with no source of income. Except for loose promises from our dad and some assistance from Aunt May, who was still living on her inheritance from her father, there was no other livelihood. As my ever quick-witted brother characterized the situation, "We are the poorest rich people there ever were."

For solace and support of a higher authority, Mom turned to the Episcopal Church in Bethel. Being a divorcée, she was denied membership. Ironically, despite that rejection, the minister, a plump, balding, married white man, had no qualms about offering my mother "Anything you want!" if only she would be his mistress. This vulgar request abruptly terminated what had been her lifelong devotion to the Episcopal Church.

The always-invincible bond between our mother, my brother, and me deepened immeasurably under the stress of our separation from the past and striking out with no anchor in sight. We regarded our mother with absolute adoration and surrounded her with our protective love. I recall with tenderness Jackie's little brown hand softly patting Mom with heartfelt understanding of the circumstances we faced. It was us, alone in an unfair world.

In June 1939, Mom, Jackie, and I moved to Danbury, Connecticut, on Lake Kenosia—a new residence, new schools, and new friends to be found. But most dramatic was our mother's new husband, James Williams Owens, a Juilliard School graduate, brown-skinned, orphaned, and seventeen years our mother's junior! This change in household had both a good and a bad side. The positive was that Owens's inherited wealth allowed our mother to continue to live in the style she had been accustomed to since her grandparents raised her. Our new home, though physically far outside the town limits, stirred considerable pride-of-residence. The long circular driveway, large wraparound porch, and light-gray stucco façade helped give the three-story, eight-room house a welcoming, Old World-style presence. Much of the eleven-acre estate

"Jowena," our home on Lake Kenosia, Danbury, CT (spring 1940)

fronted three-quarter-mile-long Lake Kenosia. The fields held wonderfully tall white birches, a grove of pine trees, grazing ground for horses, a two-stable horse barn, and a small caretaker's cottage near the entrance to the property. It was not grand, but it was quite impressive.

The grim side of our new life was the wantonly irritable disposition of Partner—the name our stepfather wanted us to call him. He was generally unpleasant to be around and gave Jackie and me a long list of house rules and restrictions, especially prohibiting us from touching his radio or turntable or any of his many musical instruments—above all, his Steinway grand piano.

Partner imposed a dramatic change in our way of life. His fancy sports cars were off limits unless we were invited to ride with him. Over the years, he acquired Porsches, MGs, Rovers, Jaguars, Rileys, and more. The collection of cars was an outgrowth of Partner's interest in advanced auto mechanics (not for personal show). Every time Jackie or I would exit one of his vehicles, he would harshly instruct, "Don't you slam that door now!" His barbed commands were a traumatic blow. "After all," Jackie protested to our mom, "aren't *we* the little royals?"

His most vexing offense was his habit of shouting at Mother. Our father, for all his shortcomings, never raised his voice to her. Daddy was respectful by nature and grandly courteous in language and gestures, even when tipsy to the point of falling over. In contrast, whenever we voiced resentment over Partner's blistering insults to our mother, he would bluntly proclaim, "All men yell at their wives!"

Infuriated, Jackie once announced to our mother, "If he doesn't stop yelling at you, *we* are going to divorce *him*!"

While Mother needed financial support, there was more to her marrying Owens than sharing his wealth. She was flattered and vindicated by the attention from this new man in her life. Among her Philadelphia girlfriends, the reaction was: "Guess what! Joe Bradford has now claimed for herself a rich, good-looking young man!" More important to our mother was her second husband's core values. He did not drink alcohol, and he was never flirtatious with other women. Perhaps most fortuitous, he came with few relatives—in other words, no in-laws.

This was quite a contrast to Mom's marriage into the Duncan clan, where her mother-in-law, Cora, had been an ever-present, aggravating critic. Cora Duncan was quite Caucasian in appearance and regularly in her travels abroad "passed" as white. Though Mom was lovely, with a coffee-cream complexion and silken black hair, the fair-skinned Cora repeatedly belittled her with, "Now they will know what we are," implying *not white*. The beautiful Josephine had been brought up in a home where fighting back or even sassing one's elders was unacceptable. Given Daddy's infidelity and hopeless drinking, she simply chose to walk away, leaving Harlem behind.

Thus, Mom's marriage to Jim Owens allowed her to alter her life's course and assume greater self-direction. Formerly a Philadelphia debutante, then the reserved wife of a prominent urban businessman, she now had the opportunity to become more self-assured in expressing herself and fun-loving in spirit. I also believe that in expanding her own personality, she attempted to set a more-becoming example for her dour husband. However, on the negative side, she found it necessary to play defensive guard for Jackie and me, protecting us from her new husband's ever-present resentment. One of Mom's repeated quotes from that time was, "I fib so much that sometimes I find myself telling the truth and I don't even know it."

Partner's bulldog expression was said to have emanated from being raised in a dull, blue-collar German family on Long Island. The presumption was that his widowed father believed a white, Bible-reading Christian clan could best raise his motherless son, regardless of their limited cultural background. The senior Owens, also named James, made a fortune as a racehorse clocker, traveling the globe timing Thoroughbreds. Among his betting victories was having "broken the bank" at the Saratoga Race Course. I remember two large leather steamer trunks stored in the basement of our Danbury home that were packed with personal effects of Partner's father. There were several exquisite gold stopwatches, jeweled cuff links, custom-made silk shirts, and well-tailored tuxedos for a slender, not very tall man. Photographs showed the senior Owens to be urbane and unsmiling.

Our stepfather's musical talent had been encouraged early in his life, as evidenced in a news-clip from his high school paper: "Please won't somebody invent a musical instrument that Jimmy Owens cannot play?" Though innately shy, he accepted without modesty that he was a born musician. On the positive side of the ledger, Partner filled the house with the wonderful sounds of symphonic recordings. Thus, it always puzzled me that a man born into the joys of music could be so wretchedly angry with everything and everyone with whom he came into contact.

My stepfather,
James W. Owens, rides
"Penny" in the pasture beside
the lake and north of our
house.

His moments of laughter were few. I do recall one rare incident when he guffawed with total delight. We had been playing a betting card game with some houseguests. I was lucky, winning pot after pot. Growing tired, I left the table to go to bed, when Partner shouted at me, "*No way* can you leave with all those winnings!" He turned to my mother and demanded, "Make her come down here, right now, to continue the game!" And indeed she did, which was no surprise, since she often importuned Jackie and me to give Partner his way, her pitiful half-smile suggesting that we should understand her plight and work with her to make a happy home. And so, I sleepily returned to the game table, eventually losing all of the chips to Partner, who gleefully gathered them close, exclaiming, "Yah! Yah! Yah! This is the way it should be!"

Such discord continued many times over until some twenty years later, when I took a firm stand against my mother's insistence that "her Jimmy" could choose his path at our expense. That time, however, my husband Clif was the victim on whom they tried to impose Partner's will. In seeking a career change and without any knowledge on our part, Owens presented himself to the leadership of the Music Department at a university where my husband was president. I personally stopped the maneuvering, which led to several very bitter exchanges between my mother and me. I don't know that she ever understood the jeopardy that the appearance of nepotism would pose to Clif's presidency. However, the underlying strength of our mother-daughter relationship allowed us to recover from the conflict. The depth of caring between the two of us was bottomless. During my last visit to her bedside before her death, my mother, with arms outstretched to embrace me, exclaimed, "My own!"

By age sixteen Jackie had grown into a most handsome fellow. He had inherited our father's green-gray eyes and our mother's beautiful hair and golden coloring. With the self-assurance of a charismatically "macho" chap, and with an innately humorous personality, my brother attracted the ladies by the score.

While attending Danbury High School, Jackie worked afternoons as a clerk in a grocery store to earn money to buy a used Cadillac convertible. The car gave him independence and the means to drive to New York City, where he stayed with our dad and socialized with longtime friends in a familiar culture. He made some friends in Danbury, but few in his age group impressed him. Jackie identified more with the achieving young Blacks in New York, Philadelphia, and Washington. He was drawn to gatherings that centered around the Penn State sports relay races, or Howard University weekend parties. No such fellowship existed in the more-provincial Danbury, and certainly none to which Jackie could relate. One of his provocative quotes was, "I'd rather be a Black somebody than a white nobody."

NEW FRIENDS

Our home on Lake Kenosia was four miles from the town and consequently did not allow me easy interaction with my classmates. Realizing that my social life was limited, Mom would invite my former New York City girlfriends to travel by train and bus to spend weekends in Danbury. But with the passing of time, those old ties began to wither. On two occasions my mom arranged for me to visit my cousins, the Fitzgeralds, in Brookline, Massachusetts. But my teen years were spent largely in Danbury, laying the foundation for adulthood that the local culture so inspired. Once again, I found myself in a place where I primarily interacted with Caucasians.

Danbury boasted several layers of middle- and upper-income families. There were prosperous factory owners and managers, Jewish entrepreneurs, and a variety of businessmen—but few, if any, women, since the prevailing expectation at that time and place was that girls "get to marry." Retail proprietors were numerous, as were doctors,

"The Radcliffe Royals," Betty and Barbara Fitzgerald. It was cousin Betty who invited me to a dorm party and introduced Clif Wharton as my blind date.

bankers, and schoolteachers, including the instructors from the local teachers college.

The children of these townsfolk became my peers upon entering Main Street School, Danbury's junior high. On my first day, Principal Clare Maginley introduced me to Anice Fript, who lived in my newly adopted residential district of Mill Plain and rode on my school bus. Anice welcomed me. Over the years, we engaged in typical teenage evaluations of what was "in" and what was "out" as we strolled along the country lane, lined by trees in a cathedral-like arch, to our respective driveway entrances. We passed the large white colonial Mason residence, whose property adjoined our own. Upon the purchase of our home, widow Mason let it be known that she was not happy about our becoming her neighbors and she did not care to meet us. I often saw the spindly, white-haired little lady weeding her garden as I walked past her home, but I never attempted to speak to her. She would turn her back to the road, willfully ignoring my presence.

Anice's father owned one of Danbury's prominent hat manufacturers. Mr. Fript shared an interest in horses with my stepfather, who always kept one or two saddle horses in the stable. They often rode around the lake together. Mother and Mrs. Fript discussed their mutual appreciation for fine table linens. She once invited Mother to join one of the local women's volunteer organizations, but Mom declined all such overtures. I suppose she did not feel the same ease of inclusion that she had with parents at the Little Red in cosmopolitan New York, where middle-class

Blacks in social settings was commonplace. Standing alone among the oft-conservative townswomen of Danbury in the early 1940s would have been a lot of weight for her to carry on a road that, for Mom, was one untraveled.

Approaching Main Street School for my first day of classes in Danbury I felt apprehension. My anxiety was not over my skin color; more worrisome was how I should behave in such an institutional environment, as compared to what I had known at the Little Red. Visually the building was bleak and joyless. Students were regimented at desks as if in a military academy. All the textbooks appeared to be exactly the same relative to each grade. Teachers stood ruler-straight in front of the students as if conducting a choir. Loud bells rang to announce room changes. While it all struck me as being unnecessarily commanding, I was excited about my advancement to junior high school and eager to find my way within the large student body. I wanted to become an insider in this, my new hometown.

I associated with many girls in Danbury's middle school and high school, but there were three with whom I bonded in friendships that continue to this day. Mary Christine Adams, whom we called Chris, was a descendant of one of the city's three founding families, going back to 1684. A second friend was Rita Feinson, whose family owned two prominent local businesses—a furniture store and a men's and ladies' department store. Marion Heyman was third among my good friends and a regular at our cafeteria lunch table.

As classmates, we shared the same homerooms, both at Main Street School and in the following years at Danbury High School. Rita, a math whiz, was far more adept at decoding my mind-puzzling algebra problems than the bored, disconnected woman who had been assigned the role of math teacher. And Chris, a literary aesthete who regaled us with quotes of her favorite authors and poets, from Shakespeare to Gertrude Stein, was always a willing consultant in reading my compositions. Though I never had any classes with Marion, her conversation revealed an astute student, less mischievous than the rest of us.

Rita, Chris, and I were not shy about approaching the high school principal, Roscoe Bassett, to discuss school matters. When we grew weary of the seemingly perpetual games of volleyball in gym classes, Rita mined the Department of Education's guidebook to assemble a list of other sports that could supplant our instructor's favored volleyball

Rita Feinson,
Chris Adams Rotello,
and I are seated on
the floating dock of
our lakeside home.
(Circa 1949)

"Danbury
Darlings," all grown
up, celebrate my
birthday at U.N.
Plaza. Left to right:
Marion Heyman,
Chris Rotello,
Rita Feinson, and
me. (July 3, 2006)

competitions. Thus armed, we petitioned our open-minded principal and were given permission to spend the remainder of that winter playing shuffleboard on the balcony above the volleyball court. On another notable occasion, we appealed to our principal one beautiful spring day to give his approval for us to "study" in the out-of-doors. With his permission, Rita, Chris, and I went to my home, where we explored the splendors of nature while sunning ourselves on my family's floating dock on Lake Kenosia.

Our romances were basically nonexistent, as there were few attractive boys worthy of our attentions. There was, however, one young student at Main Street School whose excellent mind and prep-school persona I admired. Bobby Cullerton and I often walked together in the hallways when changing classes, and we were passengers on the same school bus. There was never any dating as such, but Bobby, accompanied by his older brother, would frequently ride his bike to our home to chat awhile. His very English mother, dissatisfied with the local academic standards, was delighted when Bobby received a scholarship to a private boarding school. His departure concluded a friendship that had always sparked a playfully flirtatious smile.

I also encountered several disturbingly invisible roadblocks in this conventional New England community. Early in my Main Street School days, I was invited to attend a Girl Scouts meeting. My reception by the group was exuberant as we exchanged ideas for future meetings. Curiously, the scout director remained expressionless, speechless, and motionless when listening to our chitchat. To my surprise and disappointment, when greeting my new friends the next morning, I was informed, "Well, we're not going to be getting together as we discussed yesterday." All the plans that had been laid out so cheerfully were promptly dismissed with no explanation given. Though these same girls were congenial throughout the following high school years, our conversations never equaled the joy and buoyancy of my one and only Girl Scouts meeting. Thereafter, I have always felt disdainful of the Girl Scouts organization as delusional promoters of principled women in our society.

Another complexity in my new life involved the startup of a little social club of Danbury High School girls who happily bonded as we rotated meetings among our homes. However, after the first gathering at my house, the group never met again. Though excuses were proffered regarding this organization's cancellation, no really plausible reason was given for the termination of the club meetings. It was not until many years later, during a conversation with several longtime friends, that the stunning explanation was given by one club member's mother as saying, "When we went to Dolores's home to collect our daughters, her mother came out on the porch to greet us and, my dear, she was a *Negress!*"

Though I eagerly went on to make friends with other girls at school and on the bus, I always followed my mother's advice by responding cautiously when invited to join female-only social organizations. For years, continuing into my adult life, I was suspicious of women's groups, believing myself more secure interacting among intelligent and broadly engaged people of both sexes. Throughout life, my personal comfort zone has been where I am accepted and treated as an individual given to a wide range of interests and activities. The insider/outsider track had become a constant social consideration—and for me, most usually, a silent one.

Some positive events during the Danbury High School years were precursors to my lifetime of public speaking and love of dance. With the U.S. at war with Germany and Japan, there were ongoing support drives and campaigns wherever people gathered. When the American Red Cross was making its fund-raising appeal at the high school, Principal Bassett asked me to be the student speaker along with the Red Cross sponsors at a general assembly of all grades in the high school. I accepted, and to my amazement, the resulting praise was profuse. In continuing the drive, the Red Cross officials asked me to accompany them in walk-around tours of the high school and other local venues to spread the good word. Little did I ever imagine the countless speeches that lay ahead in my adult life. I am indebted to Danbury High School and the American Red Cross for giving me my first crack at the art of facing the public.

My second community appearance also took place in the high school auditorium. The occasion was organized by the Danbury School of Ballet for its Christmas program of Tchaikovsky's *Nutcracker.* I performed the solo in the Arabian dance suite, for which the applause was inspiring. I was delighted to be told, "I thought you were a professional brought in to elevate the show!" That was the beginning of my lifetime romance with modern dance.

But another development revolving around ballet lessons on Saturday afternoons was more complex. I had eagerly joined my high school friends in a girls' ballet class at a school on Main Street. Promptly after my second session, I was detained by the instructor, a professional ballerina, who urged me to drop the Saturday ballet class and instead take private lessons in modern dance from her after school. She claimed that the reason for suggesting the change was that my natural talent would be better served by studying modern dance—a dance form with which she admitted having had minimal training.

I couldn't help but wonder why I was being separated out from the other girls. Was the change to move me upward but at the same time out of the group? Or had the mothers intervened, as I had suspected with the Girl Scouts, to thwart my efforts to live and succeed in an all-white world? Though my being invited out of the class might have been merely a coincidence, frankly, I don't think so.

MISS ANDERSON

A counter to these hurtful episodes came about through the ordinary course of family life. Miss Marian Anderson, the renowned contralto, and her husband, architect, Razzle (a.k.a. Orpheus) Fisher, bought an estate in Danbury only three miles from our home on Lake Kenosia. My mother and Miss Anderson had been high school classmates in Philadelphia and the connection to the Fisher family was even earlier going back to the old eastern seaboard Black social connections. Upon becoming neighbors, Mom's and Miss Anderson's friendship expanded immediately. Interaction between our two households was delightfully free and open. And, extraordinary were the Fishers' invitations to their celebrity-studded week end parties for prominent artists of serious music, concert celebrities and their notable presenters such as the impresario Sol Hurok. Often when Miss Anderson was preforming in Connecticut the Fishers took us along for the outing. We would be seated backstage where I soaked up the drama of that extraordinary environment. How lovely and meaningful it was to be admitted as an insider in this a realm of real substance.

The great lady had endured many racial insults over the years, one of them of national significance. During a casual gathering in the Fishers' little TV sitting room at Marianna Farm, I heard a firsthand account of the notorious Washington incident. The Daughters of the American Revolution had denied Miss Anderson their consent to sing at DAR

Constitution Hall, then the District of Columbia's largest concert venue, citing the organization's infamous "white artists only" policy. In sober recollection of that momentous incident, Miss Anderson shook her head slowly, soulfully. My thoughts turned resentfully to the wretched failings of those petty white women who dictated arrogantly in their mindless prejudices. How dare they refuse this legendary talent!

Denied access to Constitution Hall, Miss Anderson responded by performing on the steps of the Lincoln Memorial on Easter Sunday, April 9, 1939, singing "My Country, 'Tis of Thee" before an audience of 75,000 people crowding the National Mall. The occasion was one of the most glorious moments in our nation's musical history. Through the power of her God-given musical virtuosity, Miss Anderson was the victor over the DAR's damnable racial prejudice. The great lady stood tall and proud for all the citizens of the United States.

Though Miss Anderson became an icon in the fight against racial injustice, she knew that her arduously won career and resulting fame was based on the power of her music, not on any actions as a civil rights protester or agitator. And she articulated her position informally and very clearly that evening. Furthermore, due to racism in her own country, she had to build her reputation in Europe before she was able to achieve success at home. All this despite the fact that, as the eminent British conductor Leopold Stokowski put it, "Anderson has a voice that is heard only once in a hundred years."

Marian Anderson ranks uppermost on the short list of women I consider my role models. Among the many impressions she endowed me with were her dignity and composure, presenting a pillar of strength, especially when facing the indignities of racism. On one occasion, Mom and I accompanied her on a shopping trip in downtown Danbury, to purchase fabric for her to reupholster the small sofas in their TV room (a new hobby to relax with). As we waited for service, the sales clerk cordially greeted other customers as Mrs. or Miss or Dr. and so forth. But when she finally turned to Miss Anderson, she said in a menial tone, "What do you want, *Marian*." Mom and I were infuriated, but Miss Anderson later dismissed the incident, saying it was not worth any emotional expenditure and certainly not the publicity the incident might draw. The demeanor of the salesgirl made a sharp contrast to the heartfelt ardor of thousands of admirers who would stand on line for her autograph following her concerts.

Miss Marian Anderson performs on the steps of the Lincoln Memorial in Washington, DC, before a crowd of 75,000 on April 9, 1939. *Library of Congress.*

These observations of a woman so impressively strong yet genteel as Marian Anderson encouraged me to ask myself, "So, who am I?" I had always aspired to be the "young lady" my mother wanted me to be. But then my thoughts would flip back to my Little Red School House years and the impact of educator Elisabeth Irwin's progressive teachings. My classmates and I had been taught that we were creative individuals who could be anything we aspired to be. Indeed, I was a mix of many ideas, many places, many people—even of multiple races. Knowing the nobility of Miss Anderson, I too wanted to stand my ground and to take pride in my distinctive heritage, which allows me to be uniquely myself.

CHAPTER 4

Love, Marriage, Clifton 3rd, Chicago

A BLIND DATE

My first recollection of Clifton R. Wharton Jr. was our being introduced in Harvard Yard by my cousin, Betty Fitzgerald, then a freshman at Radcliffe College. Betty had arranged for Clif to be my date, accompanying her and her escort at a formal party on the Radcliffe campus. A seventeen-year-old Harvard sophomore, Clif greeted us in The Square with a sun-bursting grin and the blooming self-confidence of a BMOC (Big Man On Campus). He had suggested that Betty and her out-of-town guest join him for a quick dinner in Adams House, his dorm, prior to the dance. A jolly threesome, Betty and I flew behind her hypersonic school chum, through The Quad, past the bronze statue of John Harvard and the venerable Widener Library, finally arriving at Clif's dorm.

Heeding house rules, Clif dropped our names into the visitors' box, then with a sweeping gesture, he ushered us into his apartment, which comprised three bedrooms, one bath, and a living room raffishly appointed with secondhand, attic-aged furnishings. The atmosphere was charged, with a half-dozen Latin American classmates mischievously exchanging barbs in Spanish, while Clif's roommates Harold May, cox of a 150-pound crew, and Carlos Blanco, a soccer star, rebutted the playful taunts of their admiring classmates. Clif, his feet always in motion even when standing in place, flipped through stacks of records, selecting the latest hit music for our entertainment.

Then we were hurried off to the cafeteria. It was a massive and noisy hall, catering to hundreds of mostly male student residents. Clif's popularity—he had just been elected production director of the Harvard

Crimson Network, the student radio station—demanded frequent absences from our table. Nonetheless, the table talk was lively, with each chap outdoing the other in exaggerated descriptions of his day. The hour spent, we rushed back across campus to Betty's house, Briggs Hall, to dress for the big evening.

In my floor-length, green taffeta gown, adorned with a white gardenia presented by my handsome escort, I was excited to be in this college setting. Though just a year younger than Clif, I was the only high school student in the room, yet I was included in the collegiate chatter, which focused on demanding courses, esteemed professors, and dormitory pranks. The prize-winning antic of the evening was about the relocation of an Adams House roommate's furnishings, which had been reassembled in the outside courtyard while he was off campus on a date. Clif threw his head back in uproarious laughter but never revealed the culprits.

As we danced together in effortless syncopation, twirling around the room in wide circles to live music, Clif surprised me, proclaiming, "Your skin is almost as pretty as mine." It took me a moment to realize he was flirting with a backhanded compliment. I feigned dismissal of his teasing, knowing the moment was mine, as if dancing with Fred Astaire in *Top Hat*.

Before bidding us goodnight, Clif asked Betty and me to attend the nine a.m. service at an Episcopal church, where he would be serving as an acolyte. We were intrigued and accepted promptly, delighted that the weekend activities would be extended with this unexpected adventure from my blind date.

Betty and I rode the elevated Red Line train to Roxbury, finally arriving at the Church of St. Augustine, which was Clif's mother's favorite house of worship. The plainly dressed, brown-skin parishioners sat solemnly in the simple chapel, with its whitewashed stucco walls and straight-back wooden chairs lined up in rows resembling pews. But splendid were the silver communion cups, candlestick holders, and crucifix as they were carried up and down the aisles by lads dressed as mini-priests.

Betty and I spoke to each other quietly—at least we thought quietly—until a small, stern British disciple of the Lord God Himself appeared before us and exclaimed in a high-pitched voice for all to hear, "How dare you speak in the house of God!" Our dignity was crushed in embarrassment. After the scolding, we, the offending intruders in this small Negro church led by an all-white clergy, did our best to conform properly:

sitting, standing, and kneeling by instruction. Though an Episcopalian myself, I found this liturgy far more complex than any I had previously practiced. However, we did slip in glances and wiggled our fingers at Clif as he strode back and forth, spreading sinuous plumes of incense throughout the chapel.

Once outside the church, Clif found us in the crowd and attempted to introduce us to his mother, Harriette Wharton, who was preoccupied conversing with other parishioners. She acknowledged the introduction, then darted off to take charge of the lingering Sunday school truants, whom she promptly marched into the church basement for their Bible lessons. Mrs. Wharton soon reappeared and, with surprising urgency, tugged at Clif's sleeve, telling him to excuse himself from Betty and me as one of her dear friends wished to see him. At that time, no one would have ever suspected that the traction exacted by Mrs. Wharton upon her son was presage of more ahead affecting my own life. With that, we knew the time had come to bid our ecclesiastic host goodbye, and a few minutes later we were on the train back to Betty's dorm for me to pack and to return home to Danbury.

The overnight at Radcliffe was my first in a residential college. The visit left me wanting to explore other institutions of higher learning so I might expand academically, make new friends, dance at dorm parties, and grow up to be a player in making the world go round. As I bade my cousin farewell, I had no suspicion whatsoever that her friend, my date Clifton Wharton Jr., would factor so fully into that life I had envisioned. But so he did, and five years later our romance became a lifelong journey and commitment.

NYU AND THE NEIGHBORHOOD PLAYHOUSE

After graduating from Danbury High School, I enrolled at New York University, whose Washington Square campus is, coincidentally, just a few blocks from the Little Red School House. Mother's inheritance from Aunt May provided funding for tuition—requiring no expenditure by my stepfather, I am pleased to say. My earliest goal was to become an English teacher, but the Western Civilization course prompted a change of major. The professor assigned myriad readings, sending us students to the stacks at the imposing Main Branch of the New York Public Library, uptown at Fifth Avenue and Forty-second Street, and the Metropolitan Museum of Art, citadels of learning I had first encountered during my Little Red years.

Alas, my career at NYU was cut short, due to a stressful call to return home. Circumstances simply had evolved in a way that left my mother completely alone in the house in Danbury. Partner was residing in New Orleans, where he was lead director of a school of music for World War II veterans, and Jackie, by this time a war veteran, was living with our dad in New York while studying to obtain his license as an undertaker. Transferring to Connecticut State University's Danbury campus appeared to be an appropriate alternative that would satisfy all my obligations.

Though the music school in New Orleans was financially rewarding, Partner was delighted when an opportunity suddenly arose allowing him a financial benefit to retire and to return home. He did not like being in the South, a sorrowful plight that all of us understood. Upon Partner's return to the homestead, I completed my coursework and promptly moved back to New York City. Since the timing of my move was unanticipated, I was out of sync in fitting back into the college semester. It was at this point that my mom urged me to enroll in the city's famed Neighborhood Playhouse. She, in turn, had been encouraged by neighbor and former theater actor/producer George Howell, who had been impressed with my speaking for the Red Cross campaign several years earlier. I honestly believe that my dear mother, who had a flair for the dramatic, was vicariously indulging her own unrealized ambitions with the possibility of my having a theatrical career.

Persuaded by her enthusiasm, I found myself under the tutelage of Sandy Meisner, celebrated teacher of method acting. The Playhouse was the training ground for some of today's thespian luminaries, such as Marian Seldes, Gregory Peck, Robert Duvall, Joanne Woodward, and countless other prominent performers and directors. Also instructing was the genius of American modern dance, Martha Graham, who was asked to introduce movement to the budding young actors by training them in her sui generis, pelvis-centered technique. My talent bloomed under her tutelage, such that I decided to linger at the Martha Graham School before returning to university.

Then fate intervened.

OUR ROMANCE

In 1949, five years after my blind date with Clifton Wharton, Betty Fitzgerald called again and asked if she might overnight with me, as she had accepted an invitation to join a "Pointer" for West Point's weekend encampment in the city. This was a surprising coincidence, as cadet Bill Woodson and I had months earlier made plans for the same weekend. Bill was an upperclassman at West Point and grandson of Carter G. Woodson, Black historian and godson of my landlady. Betty also proposed that she call her old friend Clif Wharton, by then a Manhattan resident working for Nelson Rockefeller, to ask that he assist in carrying her luggage from Grand Central Terminal to my apartment. Clif called me to make arrangements, and together he and I traveled by subway to meet Betty. The three of us returned to my apartment, where Clif promptly bade us a pleasant but casual good night. The occasion was polite, brief, and uneventful.

Separately, my cousin and I had a frolicking good time with the two cadets, who were awesomely dressed in their formal West Point uniforms. Bill Woodson attracted show-stopping attention as we waltzed around several of Manhattan's chic nightspots. On the "Pointers" final evening, Billy asked if I would accept his "A" (for army) pin, a pearl-studded gold broach. I did—partly out of respect for the young military patriots but mostly for having had several engaging outings together.

To my surprise, Clif Wharton called the very next morning and invited me out for a dinner date that evening. I consented without hesitation. Pleased with the new jewelry and having only a platonic relationship with Clif, I wore Billy's "A" pin, which Clif noticed immediately. He fingered the piece casually, turning it from side to side, then chided, "Why don't you send that pin back to that nice young man?" Clif's suggestion seemed inconsequential, but I did send it back with a letter explaining that I was not prepared to commit to the assumed intention of the pin.

Fairy tales are made to transport children into the bewitching world of wonder and happiness everlasting. The countless Prince Charmings of literature are always handsome and courageous young men who embrace maidens and make perfect their lives with kisses sweet and true. By this time, I counted myself a sophisticated New Yorker, yet I found the

Clif Wharton of 1949 to be a handsome prince who had stepped out of storybook pages of romances read long, long ago.

I was determined not to let him know that I was smitten by the depth of his intellect, his ready laughter, his wide range of choices of midtown restaurants, even his tailored suits. I readily accepted his telephone calls and cleared my calendar for his invitations, whether the dates were for a ferry ride to Staten Island, a study of the East Indian Blackbucks in the Bronx Zoo, or even a short course at the New School to review Latin American economies. There were outdoor track meets, seats at Madison Square Garden to cheer for his favorite sports teams, and dazzling stage shows. Memorable among them was an evening at the Paramount Theatre for a live performance by jazz singer Billy Eckstine. Our fun-filled days together were totally captivating. Even strangers on subway cars and strollers along Fifth Avenue would smile at us, responding to the glow of young romance.

When together, we were relieved of all family stress. New York's cultural riches offered the backdrop to our relationship, and we embraced the city wholeheartedly. We delighted in having the liberty to choose among our various friends of all ethnic, cultural, and religious backgrounds. Life became an ongoing, thoroughly enjoyable ballet of pleasant entrances and exits, of movies, museums, concerts, and theater.

Eventually I decided it was time to present Clif to my family. Several years before, during one of Clif's summers at Camp Atwater, he had met my stepfather, then a counselor at a recreational camp in North Brookfield, Massachusetts, for middle- and upper-class Blacks. Consequently, Partner's dour disposition during Clif's visit to Danbury was neither a surprise nor an impediment to the weekend. Mother was typically gracious, as she was with most of my beaus. This time, however, she offered no undercutting quips following the visit, as was her practice to eliminate those whom she wished me to dismiss.

Marriage remained a casual topic of conversation, with Clif giving me a rundown of the things—if and when he married—he expected his wife to be. His list was so detailed that I quipped, "It sounds as if you need a Sears and Roebuck catalogue to order up a mate."

It was no longer than eight months, filled with our lighthearted jaunts in and around New York City, before Clif concluded he neither needed nor wanted to consider any further search for a wife. One lovely late afternoon, when we were sitting on a bench in the Rockefeller Center complex, a frequent meeting place before we would take off on our many excursions, my Prince Charming proposed. The world went silent during that very precious moment as Clif Wharton, his face leaning into mine, whispered, "Dolores, will you marry me?"

Quietly, and with tenderest sentiment, I said, "Yes."

CLIF'S PARENTS

One evening, when I returned to the apartment where I was staying with my best friend, Mary Carmen Aldridge, Clif surprised me, arriving unexpectedly with his father, Clifton R. Wharton Sr. The distinguished gentleman was a noted diplomat who later became the first Black career ambassador. He was making a quick trip back to the United States from his current post as deputy chief of mission in Lisbon.

My hair was horribly windblown, having just walked across the 138th Street Bridge, plus I was hungry and tired after a day of tedious desk work at Abercrombie and Fitch, where I was temporarily employed. A few days after the unforeseen visit, I asked Clif, "Why didn't you tell me you were bringing your dad to meet me?"

"I wanted him to see you just as you are," he replied.

My inner voice rebelled, saying, "No, Dolores, more like the Old Darling met you at your worst!" But I need not have worried; Clif's father and I became fondly simpatico in a relationship that stretched devotedly through the years.

Clif's mother was a very different matter. A devout Bostonian, Harriette Wharton possessed the personality of an unsmiling sovereign in command of her younger children: William, Richard and Mary. Alas, she had recently become a very sad woman. Two years prior to my appearance, her husband had asked for a divorce. The last thing she now wanted was another woman interrupting her dismally changing life. And that, I believe, is how she perceived me for many years—a complex distraction stepping between her and her revered eldest son.

While I feel it is inappropriate to go into the troubling incidents between my mother-in-law and me, our mutual displeasure with each other permeated the courtship and early years of my marriage. There is an analogy that offers a fitting comparison. President Franklin Roosevelt's mother maintained inseparable ties to her son, and her deflating demands upon her daughter-in-law, Eleanor, are well documented. The matriarch's criticism is an excellent analogy for Harriette Wharton's determination to instruct me in what she believed to be her own exemplary manner of thinking, behaving, and most essentially caring for her eldest son.

I deeply regret that she and I were not friends. Begrudging tolerance became the sole channel allowing a viable relationship; that is, until it became obvious that the strength of Clif's and my happy marriage was key to the success of his future career. Harriette Wharton finally accepted me many years later, when Clif became president of Michigan State University and I became the university's First Lady. As I served in that role, she came to recognize my social skills and cultural breadth, knowing these qualities to be essential in her son's wife.

THE WEDDING

One winter's afternoon in December 1949, while Mom and I were engrossed in planning my wedding, Razzle Fisher dropped by to catch up on neighborly chitchat. The major concern of the moment was where to hold the ceremony. Given Mom's divorce, the Episcopal Church was not an option.

Mr. Fisher gave the situation some thought, then proposed, "Well, Dolores could be married in Marian's studio."

Mom and I were totally thrilled by the suggestion, and I declared, "Being married in Miss Anderson's studio would be fabulous!"

As we discussed the details, Mr. Fisher recommended that the number of guests not exceed fifty people, explaining, "The space is too small for more than that."

Thus, my wedding to Clif was held in Marian Anderson's studio on her estate, Marianna Farm, set among the beautifully rounded hilltops of Connecticut, on Saturday afternoon, April 15, 1950.

And while we aimed to limit the gathering to fifty guests, oh, my dear, it expanded to at least double the number. The wedding was regarded as a major social event of the season. Dr. C. B. Powell, a constant friend of the Duncan family and owner of the *Amsterdam News*, asked his paper's lead Harlem social columnist to give our wedding priority coverage. Geri Major, armed with a photographer and the guest list, faithfully filled two pages recounting who attended, and what they were wearing for the occasion.

Miss Marian Anderson kisses the bride. (April 15, 1950). *Amsterdam News*, April 22, 1950

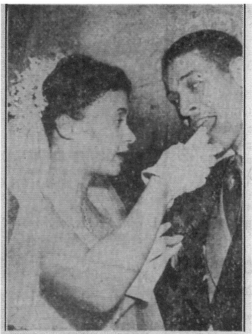

THE FIRST piece of cake cut at the wedding is given to the groom by the bride. The reception was held in the Marian Anderson studio in Danbury, Conn. It was the season's major wedding.

The beginning of our sweet life together. *Amsterdam News*, April 22, 1950

Throughout history, weddings have been the subject of dramas, comedies, financial extravagances, and legendary indignities. Mine was no exception. The one incident for which I have yet to forgive my mother was her delaying the ceremony for a solid hour, leaving a hundred people who had gathered from all points along the Eastern Seaboard waiting jam-packed in Miss Anderson's beautiful studio. It turned out that she, when collecting Partner's rented morning-frock suit, appropriate for giving the bride away, had left behind the crucial formal necktie. Therefore, minutes before the wedding was scheduled to begin, she sent a driver into the midst of Danbury's horrendous Saturday afternoon traffic to fetch the necktie. I was distressed and outraged—after all, she could have dressed him in one of his ridiculous clip-on bow ties, and nobody would have known the difference. Humiliated, I locked myself in the bathroom to cry for the hour. Mary Aldridge, my matron-of-honor, was the one person I allowed to be with me, and she posted a note on the bathroom door: "No Admittance—Miss Bride Is Contemplating."

Then came one surprisingly sweet pause in my anguish. My mother tapped at the bathroom door and said, "Dolores, your father is on the phone. He wants to speak with you."

I hurried to take the call. My dad spoke softly and tenderly, saying, "I would love to be with you today, Baby, but that's not possible, so I am calling on your wedding day to wish you deepest happiness in your marriage. And I want you to always remember, Baby, that Daddy loves you."

My father's endearing words quieted my distraught emotions, and upon returning to the bathroom, I asked Mary to leave the door unlocked.

With Felix Mendelssohn's "Wedding March" resounding at full volume, the bridal procession finally began. Willing away all anxieties, I walked arm-in-arm with my mother's second husband to meet Clif at the beautifully assembled, blossom-laden altar. At that moment, Clif's eyes possessed mine, uniting us in a utopian lifetime journey that has kept us joyfully together for seven decades.

Two priests officiated at the ceremony: Father Bishop, whose history with both my parents and the Duncan Brothers business was extensive, and Harriette Wharton's Father Dale of Boston's Church of St. Augustine. There was soft sobbing by both our mothers, and loud wailing from someone standing among the groom's ushers. It was my dear brother, Jackie, caught up in the sentimentality of giving up his little sister to marriage. Later, Clif's grandmother, Mary Hicks, quietly approached

Jackie and whispered in his ear, "Don't be concerned, our Clifton will take good care of your sister."

Cheerful rejoicing prevailed into the evening, with an intimate dinner in our home on Lake Kenosia and the traditional clamor of wedding festivities, which overflowed with affectionate embraces, sparkling bubbly, and fancy cakes. The sun finally set as the bride and groom slipped out into the world alone together and blissful in life's promise.

TWO YEARS LATER

The date was September 4, 1952. During the prior summer, the buzz at Riverton, a residential development in Harlem that was our first residence in New York, was, "Dolores Wharton is walking around as if possessed in a dream world for pregnant women." But reality set in immediately upon returning home with our eight-pound-two-ounce baby boy who, for three full weeks, refused to be put down in his blue-skirted bassinet. He was besieged with colic, and we with sleeplessness. Clif and I ran what seemed like an around-the-clock marathon, with one of us walking the floors carrying the crying babe while the other raced back to bed to catnap.

But the joy of parenthood was so all-absorbing that our hearts were impervious to the wearying demands of a newborn. I adored the countless new wonders of him: his sweet baby smell, his funny noises, his feet kicking the air, his recognizing us! Having a child should never, ever be regarded as "stuff happens." Every child deserves to be wanted. Clif and I deeply wanted Clifton 3rd and his brother, Bruce, who was born in 1959. Their arrivals were the advent of looking at life totally anew.

THE UNIVERSITY OF CHICAGO

Clif's four years as a graduate student at the University of Chicago produced a superb econometrician and an intellectual savant. His demanding studies and part-time employment required that both our lives be bound within the university environs. Clif's assignment as a research assistant to Dr. Theodore Schultz, working on a Latin American study, provided our livelihood. Equally important, his job offered constant in-depth interaction within the exalted department of "Chicago economics"—nationally respected for its mathematical orientation, superstar professors, and distinguished graduate student body. Not to minimize Clif's earlier academic performances—after all, he stood tall as an undergraduate at Harvard and in his master's degree studies at Johns Hopkins School of Advanced International Studies. But Chicago was his greatest and most rigorous intellectual challenge. It was where he became a true scholar.

Already among Clif's personal qualities was his inherent leadership ability. Fellow students and friends turned to him with ready and easy endorsement, as exemplified in such achievements as:

Captain of the track team, Boston Latin School;
Production Director, Harvard Crimson Network;
Outstanding primary school cadet, Tuskegee Army Air Program;
Co-chairman, New England Student Christian Conference;
Harvard delegate to the U.S. National Student preliminary
    conference;
National secretary, U.S. National Student Association founding
    convention;
President, graduate student Economics Club University of Chicago

Added to Clif's obvious accomplishments was a beguiling personality that was at once engaging and disarming. On the surface, he used his sense of humor playfully in making friends, but underneath was the strength of a serious force to be reckoned with and interests capable of enriching a changing society. He could have contributed well as a politician, adding enormously to the leadership of our Black people. But I am grateful to the powers-that-be that his scholarly interests predominated, leading him into the world of higher education.

Social gatherings at the U of C ranged from the professors' at-home receptions for students and spouses to the ultracasual bring-a-dish gatherings among the grad-student families in our respective homes. Regardless of venue, hospitality was all-embracing. However, when dining with Clif's fellow students, I had to listen-up attentively, as economists use a specialized vocabulary and have a proclivity to duel as warriors, constantly sparring to prove one's point.

We lived at 1121 East 60th Street in one of the university's little World War II prefabricated bungalows situated on the Midway, one block from the boys dormitory Burton-Judson. Just a few steps from our door were some two hundred other graduate student families, with children, pets, and budgets as limited as ours.

Outside our prefab house at the University of Chicago, Clifton 3rd in his dad's academic mortarboard admires a recent diploma. (August 1956)

At ten months, young Clifton, an exceptionally long child who grew to be six-foot-four, was still crawling on all fours. But by age two he became a hobbyhorse jockey alongside a neighbor's little girl, Chiori, a Nisei (Japanese American) who lived directly across the cinder path from us. Clifton 3rd also was a devoted, card-carrying member of the neighborhood library. He and I traveled by bicycle all around Hyde Park, his legs dangling from cutout openings in a large metal basket attached to the handlebars.

Our favorite afternoon destination was the Museum of Science and Industry, where we toured exhibits of new technical inventions and stunning discoveries. Another playtime excursion was to the beach on Lake Michigan just off 60th Street, where we swam, played ball and tag, and delighted in the hot Chicago sun. When Clifton 3rd was three, we entered him in a morning nursery school, where I spent two months "on the bench" watching him play with other three- and four-year-olds until he finally adjusted to the new setting. For his fourth birthday party, young Clifton proudly delivered his own invitations. His earliest years were spent within the graduate student world, where language was so inadvertently influenced by academic lingo that we were not too surprised when his guests' parents told us he had delivered the invitations with the announcement, "Here is my dissertation to my fourth birthday party!"

Our household budget was $15 a week, which included groceries, spirits, and cigarettes. I rode my bicycle-with-basket to the supermarket until the inheritance from my dad's estate made it possible for us to afford a secondhand car. Clif reserved Saturday mornings to assist me with grocery shopping. Once, to our great dismay, while checking out, we dropped a gallon jug of Zinfandel. This would have provided a week's supply of joyful imbibing—our one indulgence—but alas, there was no replacement forthcoming, as we were on the wrong side of the cash register, making the calamity all our own. Despite the hardships, I look back fondly on that period as being especially rewarding, having forged uniquely strong and compatible relationships with other families struggling to reach the same goal: those hard-earned and preciously coveted PhD degrees.

During this period, I was invited to become a member of the Dames Club, a national organization of the wives of graduate students. (Upon the husband's graduation with a PhD, the Dame is awarded her PHT, which is transposed to "Putting Hubby Through.") We met on campus in beautiful Ida Noyes Hall, which offered meeting rooms and comfortable lounges for female students and was located directly adjacent to our home on the Midway. During meetings, we enjoyed the practice of British-style pouring of a proper tea and listened to guest scholars.

I was especially pleased to be asked to join a small bridge group of professional women whose husbands were professors in Clif's Department of Economics. The invitation began with Professor Gary Becker asking if I would like to join his and his colleagues' wives in playing bridge. I was tickled to accept and doubly flattered, since I was a newcomer to the game and the only student wife to be invited. I enjoyed our informal gatherings and especially conversation with women of such academic and professional achievement, whose primary concentration was the art of the game. We held regular evening meetings in one another's homes, and I remained in the group until Clif finished his studies and we left the university. I became addicted to the challenge of bridge, and delighted in being an insider among these accomplished and really interesting women.

During our four years at Chicago, there were people whom I respected and enjoyed—and, only rarely, others whom I purposefully ignored. There was but one caller at our prefab who forced me to suppress anger as I thought to myself, "Watch what you say, Dolores, there's a potential racial problem here!" I had observed this neighbor in our common laundry shed and had exchanged only controlled half-smiles. She had bulging hips, beehive blonde hairdo, and a cornpone Southern accent that seemed to thicken as she stood at my door and asked if I might know of someone who would clean her bungalow. I knew full well that she had me in mind. On silently hearing her out, I restrained myself from spewing red-hot words of anger. Instead, I didn't respond to her request and abruptly concluded the conversation, saying I needed to depart immediately to pick up little Clifton, who was away on a play date. I then audibly shut the door. Dismissing the intruder's implied insult, I forgave her as a stupid white woman who just didn't know any better. Then I grabbed my coat and hurried off to collect my son.

Beyond that, there were no other memorable racial insults. On a few occasions when walking about the campus, I caught glances from squinted eyes flashing with the insinuation, "What are *you* doing here?" But such slights were in sharp contrast with my interactions in the community, and consequently easy to dismiss as irrelevant. The University of Chicago was a large campus of brilliant, progressive people, where small minds and petty acts had no place.

There were moments when I thought myself a weakling unable to say "No!" Such was the case when Erwin "Bud" Beyer, a gymnastics coach and the founding director of Acro-Theater, implored me to choreograph a theatrical production of student gymnasts. There was no leisure time in my schedule. Besides, gymnastics is not an art form, but a sport! Yet I realized that my training under Louis Horst, master choreographer of the Martha Graham School, had provided me with the skills to bring modern dance into the productions that Coach Beyer wanted Acro-Theater to offer. As a Graham disciple eager to share my knowledge of her technique, I followed through, working with the students on dance creations over two consecutive years.

The theater group offered me two very welcome opportunities. One was to get physically into shape again, as my muscles were simply not awake for me to work with. My answer was to enroll in a U of C dance program. And, secondly, the joy was in revisiting my longtime passion for dance. As a consequence, I had a lovely stretch of time beyond my routine responsibilities, leaving me quite pleased for having accepted the role as the modern-dance choreographer of Acro-Theater.

I had always intended to complete my undergraduate degree, and now it seemed possible. I would love to have attempted matriculation at the University of Chicago, but the U of C tuition for the two of us was prohibitive. Besides, my family needed my attention. After some research, I determined that Chicago State University offered the most accommodating combination of night courses and it would accept enough transfer credits from NYU and Connecticut State to give me upper-level status. Clif was happy to care for Clifton in the evenings while he studied at home, allowing me time for night school. The coursework was enjoyable—even ego boosting, thanks in part to Clif showing me ingenious economists' numbers tricks that helped me achieve stellar grades in subjects I had once found forbidding. Being a mature student I grasped at education more intensely, actually benefitting academically from the richness of a fuller life from the past.

One last hurdle sprang up in the months just prior to completing my coursework. Clif was importuned to start his new job in New York City right away, as the need for his involvement was immediate. Once again, I was abruptly required to leave my studies behind, and it was several years before I resumed. With the submission of a research paper on the Edo Period of Japanese art, I received a degree in Art History from Chicago State University. Many years later, in recognition of my work designing a program to enhance the upward mobility of young women and minorities in corporate America, Chicago State awarded me an Honorary Doctor of Humane Letters. Life had come full circle.

As our family left campus in 1957 in our gray Chevrolet, we stopped at the U of C bookstore and bought the revered volumes of the Classical Humanities. These books became remembrances of our time in Chicago and a stimulus for further home studies—treasures that I carried faithfully back to Manhattan.

Our return to New York was for only a brief stint. Arthur T. Mosher, an economist heading the Council on Economic and Cultural Affairs (a foundation of John D. Rockefeller 3rd that focused on rural development in Asia, later named the Agricultural Development Council, or ADC), brought Clif onto his team with the title Council Field Associate. But before taking up his assignment in Asia, Clif needed to complete his doctoral thesis. Art Mosher was critically supportive, giving Clif leave status while he finished writing his dissertation at home.

No longer students, rather, we were a typical middle-class family of three. Still, we were cautious with our finances. Rather than spend money on a proper desk, my handy and ingenious husband sandpapered and varnished a wooden board, which he rested on the arms of a comfortable

Clifton 3rd, right, stands tall with my brother's three children: Jackie IV and twins Bradford Duncan and Barbara. (1958)

brown-velvet armchair, creating a large-enough desktop at which he spent much of the year writing.

Being back in New York City also allowed a reconnection with my brother. Now a licensed undertaker, Jackie, was sole owner and director of Duncan Brothers Funeral Home and husband to a show-stopping beauty, Ann Thorne. They had three adorable children, John W. Duncan IV and twins Bradford and Barbara, whom our young Clifton could not visit often enough.

By taking up residence again in the Riverton apartments in Harlem, we could afford the full tuition for Clifton 3rd to attend private school. At Ethical Culture, young Clifton, ever spontaneous and energetic, adjusted easily to his highly self-assertive classmates in the classrooms, on field trips, and at play dates throughout the school year. A strong believer in keeping little people busy, I also sent him to summer day camp, which admittedly he hated—"enough already, Mom!" he declared.

On August 29, 1958, we three flew back to Chicago, where Clif marched in the procession at the Rockefeller Chapel of the University of Chicago to receive that all-meaningful PhD degree, affording him the honorific Chicago Economist—a diploma that young Clifton owned as much as his dad.

The next stop for our little family was in Southeast Asia, which would prove to be a colossal life changer, made more so by our having a second child on the way. I packed and re-packed every treasured possession acquired over our eight-year marriage into two large steamer trunks, while storing our large upholstered furniture in a warehouse for the duration of our time away from the United States.

The expectation was that we were to embark on a ten-year mission to a world that was totally unfamiliar to me. Using every possible channel and recommendation, I educated myself about Asia. I scouted through *The New Yorker* magazine's listings of documentary films, subscribed to *National Geographic* and *Life,* read all of Pearl Buck's novels, bowed with hands clasped to courteous hosts in Chinese and Japanese restaurants. I knew very well that my efforts were limited. The one truly valuable resource was conversations with professionals who were knowledgeable and well-traveled in the region. Phillips Talbot and his wife, Mildred, gave me the most in-depth understanding of what to expect in our new adventure. An ADC trustee, Phil was an esteemed scholar and envoy in the region—especially India, where he had met Mildred when she worked for the CIA.

Mildred tried to persuade me that "Anything you use in New York City will be available to you in Singapore," and, "What the locals covet most are clever American novelties." She advised me to "Go shopping for some fun gifts for your new hosts. Asians are big on gift-giving, and you will need to reciprocate." Mildred added, "I took wine bottle openers with dangling mink tails to India on our last trip, and they were a big hit!" Along with this useful trivia, our exchanges with the Talbots led to volumes of serious and enriching conversations that extended for over forty years.

At last we three, with Bruce just weeks from arriving, flew to Singapore. There we would grow as we reached out to the exotic worlds of Asia with their different languages, religions, customs, cuisines, and preferences. Little did I realize that my worldview, which had accepted Western civilization as all-encompassing, would be lifted to Star Wars heights with the revelations of Southeast Asia's diverse and deeply engaging cultures.

CHAPTER 5

Singapore and Malaysia

Descending the aircraft steps in Singapore, we were met with merciless humidity and a grinning hot sun that attacked my poor bedraggled body, bulging with unborn Bruce, and squeezed every ounce of energy left after the long flight from New Delhi. Who was there to greet us on the tarmac? A stunning Chinese airport hostess, exquisitely dressed in a knockout powder-blue *cheongsam* dress with side slits thigh-high. She greeted us with a smile and said to my handsome husband and our six-year-old son, "Please follow me!"

Totally drained, I clumped awkwardly behind them. This was my introduction to the devouring climate and the gorgeous Asian women who were obviously able to dismiss the life-sapping physical environment while radiating a guileless sexuality. Should I catch the next plane back to New York City? Not on your life! I had left behind my mother's loving maternal care, a comfortable climate, and a culture I totally understood. Instead, I became bewitched with the exciting adventures Southeast Asia promised: Chinese, Malays,[1] and Indians with their unique color preferences and amazing ethnic cuisines; the sounds of calls to prayer from mosques; the click-clacking of bamboo sticks announcing hawkers with a whole department-store of household wares overflowing atop their spindly bicycles. And oh, all the bicycles—hundreds, thousands of them!

I was speechless for months as if standing still among a trillion multicolored jigsaw pieces that floated in the air and eventually settled around me. Every step I took, turn I made, sight, sound, aroma I absorbed was a

---

1   Malays are members of the Malay ethnic group, the largest in Malaysia. Malaysians are citizens of Malaysia, regardless of their ethnicity.

strange and intoxicating blend of wondrous things. Each morning during our six-year residence in Singapore and Malaysia[2] brought the promise of some new and intriguing experience to ponder. I had learned at the Little Red School House that through direct interaction with a community, one could learn well and richly, and thus it was with that promise I fully embraced this new adventure.

Singapore proffered a cacophony of sensations that filled not only my ears but my entire being. Add the visuals of storefronts with Chinese calligraphy or ornately curved Sanskrit contrasted with flat English lettering, and the ambiguity was dazzling. The shrill calls for "Money change! Money change!" and "How much you pay?" in local currency "change alleys" made you wonder what deals or opportunities you were missing by a second of inattention. Food and fruit stands were everywhere; even on the outskirts near residential buildings and construction sites, one would hear vendors by their pushcarts hawking savory noodles, spicy buns, exotically prepared meat and fish.

As field associate for the Council on Economic and Cultural Affairs, Clif's regional responsibilities were in Singapore, Malaysia, Thailand, and Vietnam. He also served as visiting professor at the University of Malaya and as senior executive making grants and contributions for research projects in the emerging Southeast Asian colleges, universities, and governments. And he identified scholars in these institutions for graduate doctoral study to become Council Fellows in the United States. During our two years in Singapore, he taught several economics courses, which continued at the university in Kuala Lumpur following our move to Malaysia's capital city. There he added wide-ranging research studies dealing with local farm issues, utilizing his students to count everything and anything economists love to count.

Mrs. Brown, Clif's office assistant in Singapore, was an English expat housewife with good secretarial skills and a touch of the old missionary zeal. She insisted on taking young Clifton 3rd to her Baptist church services every Sunday morning, I believe out of concern for the absence of "real" Christian teachings in our Episcopalian household. Many years later, Clifton 3rd became a practicing Buddhist, informing us somewhat accusingly, "Don't blame me! It was you who exposed me to the multiple

2 During most of our stay, Malaysia was officially called the Federation of Malaya; the name Malaysia was not adopted until 1963. I have used the current name Malaysia, except in the names of organizations and places that use Malaya.

religions of Asia." I suspect that Mrs. Brown scared him by causing conflict between her Baptist and our Episcopalian faiths. So, what could he do otherwise? Knowing Clifton's mind, embrace a "Middle Way" and become a Buddhist, of course.

Our home was a 1950s two-story bungalow set beside a traditional *kampong* (Malaysian village) on a quiet Singapore hillside. Living in an attached house was a middle-class Chinese family whose patriarch could be seen on his patio before sunrise every morning, stretching in Tai Chi exercises. But his two young sons played outside only after the sun's rays had dipped in late afternoons. (It was whispered that tanning was strongly avoided among the "high born" classes.)

On the opposite side of our road, Malay children and men gathered in the early evening to play *sepak raga*, a kickball game that produced streams of uproarious laughter among the players. The men and boys wore sarongs over skinny hips, the tiny tots seldom wore anything at all. Nearby, women in pleated skirts and overhanging blouses busied themselves domestically, shooing away chickens that pecked aimlessly underfoot. We waved to our *kampong* neighbors, happily coming under the spell of the syncopated music that flew gently from their portable radios.

Another frequent marvel observed from our patio were long funeral processions that weaved their way along the neighboring hilltop. At the front were twenty or more professional mourners dressed in white garments and pointed hats, banging drums, clapping cymbals, and chanting incantations to chase away evil spirits. The trailing family members carried banners with farewell salutations and photographs of the deceased looking stern in their finest attire. This was a Chinese ritual, as noisy and almost as melodramatic as roadside Chinese opera, and quite a contrast to the services at Duncan Brothers Funeral Home.

Our family's domestic routine was for me life-changing. Both in Singapore and Kuala Lumpur there was the glorious support from several loyal household servants. Our first *amah*, or maid, was Ah Tai, who had been reared in the Black and White Amahs sisterhood, a Cantonese group sworn to celibacy, hard work, and loyalty. These women took their name from their customary attire of long, wide-bottom black silk pants and crisp, white cotton tops. Today there are few from that unique professional order still living.

Ah Tai lived in our home with a single day off each week. Late one afternoon, I was surprised to see her preparing to depart for an off-schedule

Bruce and Yap Joon Foo, his steadfast caregiver
(Singapore, 1959)

Ah Tai, Bruce, and me (Singapore, 1959)

overnight. Her absence would leave little Clifton and me—then nine months pregnant—alone, as Clif was out-of-country on a field trip. Since newly independent Singapore was in the midst of the island nation's first autonomous election, I stoically and sincerely commended Ah Tai on her commitment to cast a ballot for the next prime minister.

"Oh, no," she replied tartly, "I'm not going to vote. If you are still here in the morning"-by which she meant to say, *Not forced out by a rioting mob*-"I'll come back."

The next morning Clifton 3rd and I were delighted to find the table set for breakfast. Ah Tai, unrepentant, had returned to our residence as the election went peacefully and swiftly, too. The launching of Lee Kuan Yew's remarkable leadership as prime minister had begun.

When it was time for Bruce to join the family, he arrived without customary announcement—urgently in fact! As a consequence, in the rush to sign him in at the Seventh-day Adventist hospital our little newborn got listed in the local records as Chinese and a Singapore citizen. Before the official ink had time to dry, my good husband dashed into the American Consulate General and registered Bruce as American, requesting that he be issued his very own passport. Other than my breaking out in bright red hives, Bruce and I were made perfectly comfortable at the hospital, except that I would have preferred a lot less of the Seventh-day Adventist meatless menus. It was tofu-everything for a week.

Finally relaxed at home with our cherubic babe, Clif, Clifton 3rd, and certainly I took great comfort with our newly hired second *amah*, Yap

The centerpiece of my happy life: Clif at play with Clifton 3rd and Bruce in Malacca

Joon Foo, whose single responsibility was the care, especially at night, of baby Bruce. Joon's clan was different from Ah Tai's. As Joon was younger and less formal, she preferred not to use the honorific "Ah" ascribed to her station. We simply called her Joon. Ah Tai and Joon spoke different Chinese dialects, but they understood English well and were fluent in Malay, as was the Indian gardener, Romian. Our household was multiracial, multilingual, and we were multi-cared for.

Among her many attributes, Joon possessed one quality beyond measure—she attended to our little son as though he were her own. She even schooled him in a few Chinese customs; one memorable example: within her clan, every household member was expected to contribute to its overall operations. So, by six months Bruce had learned an important lesson. Upon arriving at our breakfast table one morning, Joon, with Bruce in her arms, his wet diaper pail dangling from his little fingers, announced, "You see, Bruce has a job, too!"

To complete the intimacy of our home, "Big Daddy" Clif purchased a Grundig radio with record player console, giving flight to the recordings of Duke Ellington, Glenn Miller, Count Basie, Erroll Garner, and the Chico Hamilton Quintet—music that brought a bit of familiarity to balance our newly adopted home.

With my house in order, I could stretch out into our new life with exuberance. Art Mosher, the Council's visionary leader and Clif's boss, supported us spouses by providing travel expenses so we could attend

Council meetings and conferences in Asia. Consequently, I had the luxury of being a journeyman alongside Clif, observing the richness of vastly different cultures during his visits to Asian universities. I became well acquainted with Clif's colleagues and with local aides whom Clif engaged in his research projects. Extending myself, with Art Mosher's encouragement, I became Clif's full partner. Be they meetings held in the host university offices, regional field stations, or our Singapore or Kuala Lumpur residences, I was overjoyed to engage in knowledgeable conversation with his international peers. But also my participation was more than useful, it was regarded as important to Clif's operations in the field. This ongoing interaction with the professionals in his regional activities provided a valuable practice for Clif's and my joint efforts in later life.

There were countless visitors to be welcomed to our home, including Clif's stateside colleagues in higher education, other international foundation executives, and business leaders exploring Asia for the first time—some accompanied by their wives. Many unseasoned travelers arrived panting from exhaustion, just as we had. I soon created my own Confucian saying: "Take long sleep after flying around globe." To be honest, this was not Confucian but a little "Dolores-Speak". I would remain patient, until the overwhelmed visitors were ready to embark on my sightseeing tours, which included such customary venues as Hindu and Buddhist temples and the famed Batu Caves.

But there also were more adventuresome outings. We splashed through wet floors of open markets, where one could see gigantic green sea turtles and twenty-foot-long pythons hung by their heads, awaiting the butcher's knife to slice thick meaty steaks. We wandered through arboretums lush with carnivorous plants transplanted from Borneo and elephantine-ear trees that formed a canopy under which hordes of impish monkeys screamed mockingly at visitors. Roadside vendors sold us exotic fruits, including the foul-smelling durian, reputed to be an aphrodisiac, which inspired an amusing little ditty: "When the durian comes to town, the skirts go up and the pants go down."

We stepped inside curio shops selling flawless apple-green jade and prized pink quartz jewelry; stared at sidewalk pharmacies stocked with preserved animal genitals and rhinoceros ivory, promising infallible medical remedies; and despaired over forgotten, baldheaded old folk glaring from windows of dilapidated buildings known as "death houses." There was the "little India" district, crowded with shops displaying brilliant silks, cotton rugs, handsomely woven baskets, and spices that burned our nostrils as we strolled past. On one notorious nighttime tour, we drove by a row of brothels so unusually busy that the owner was heard announcing, "No massagee, fucking only!"

CULTURE AND IDENTITY

In Singapore, I let my guest-shoppers run loose at C.K. Tang, a Chinese department store that offered beautifully embroidered linens and every kind of domestic paraphernalia made in mainland China. Also, for tourist and celebrity guests alike, I would personally escort them to the museums and art galleries, showing off the young talents of Singapore and Malaysia. Most visitors were fascinated and found colorful canvases of fine artistic merit to take back home. I completed my tours with a welcome return to our tranquil domicile, with twirling ceiling fans and fresh lime drinks served by Ah Tai dressed in her black-and-white outfit, slippers flip-flopping on the cool marble floors.

Our professional grounding was mainly among the faculty on the Singapore and Kuala Lumpur campuses of the University of Malaya, where Clif's teaching base was established. Though the faces of the academic population were quite new to us—Chinese, some Indian, a few Malays, and a heavily British teaching staff—social interaction was very much as expected. Our acceptance by scholars, administrators, and students was more formal—a natural mien among the British-trained. But it was as congenial a lifestyle as we had known at the University of Chicago.

In Asia, Clif's and my racial identity was simply "American," with no further delineation. We Americans are conspicuous by our deportment, despite racial variations. We can't help it—it's a fact—people the world over can easily spot us as "Yanks" regardless of our skin color. Furthermore, coloration in Singapore and Malaysia is far more varied than in the United States. In studying all aspects of these amazing people, I found that the Chinese came in a wider range of hues varying from flawless ivory among the ladies of leisure to the ruddy brown of sun-laboring farmers; the Malays were cast in a smooth, warm tan widely found throughout the Malaysian peninsula and Indonesia; the Indians' coloration stretched from pale primrose to solid jet black, their silken, glossy hair considered the finest by wigmakers around the globe. With these dominant racial characteristics among the multiple societies in which we were living, Clif's and my ethnicity was a non-issue in the broad mix of things.

I wish the same could be said for everyone from my own country. There was one pitiful racial incident involving a visiting white American economist from the U.S. Department of Agriculture, who was guest of honor at a lovely dinner party given by a Malay government official. The other guests were local economists and their wives—Chinese, Indian, and English. All of us were properly dressed for dinner—men in dark suits, the ladies in evening silks—that is, except the guest of honor, who wore a sporty, casual outfit. Upon leaving the table, we gathered for coffee in the orchid-filled garden, where the visitor asked if he might share an after-dinner custom of his southern American homestead: country music! He broke forth in a booming voice, "Carry me back to Old Virginny!" After each refrain, he would throw back his head and, with emotional emphasis, soulfully exclaim, "Dere'z where dis old darky's heart am long'd to go!" On and on he continued in a feigned Negro dialect about "dis old darky."

Finally, the song concluded, the other guests applauded, flashing side glances at Clif and me. We remained expressionless, absent any gesture of appreciation. Simultaneously, Clif and I stood, thanked our hosts for the joy of being in their home—and then, with no recognition of the performer, we promptly departed. The insult had been simply and unequivocally registered.

Clif and I were appalled! The honored guest's performance had been a display of blatant racism by an American official serving that evening as an exporter of American bigotry. His song portrayed the Black people of our country as dim-witted, illiterate, amusingly childish, and generally inferior. The man was a guest in Malaysia, a former British crown colony that had recently won independence from a ruling empire that had considered the Malay people as inferiors. Clif and I had been welcomed in Malaysia, where Clif exemplified the finest of American higher education and professional excellence, sharing his academic prowess to further the development of rural social sciences throughout Southeast Asia.

Years later, Clif received a letter of polite contrition from that visiting American official. He said he regretted the possible insinuation between the hapless old Negro in his song and us. Even in apologizing, it was clear that he still didn't "get it."

We made great good friends within the university community. Several families became central to our lives in Singapore and later in Kuala Lumpur. We were in perfect sync with the Hendricksons—John, the father, a professor in the Department of Zoology, his wife Lupe, and their four children—youngsters we found to be the finest role models of American children reared abroad. Their son Mark became young Clifton's best friend. The boys romped with abandon during overnight stays in each other's homes.

We were frequently invited to both the Singapore and Kuala Lumpur homes of Ungku Aziz, a Malay nobleman who was revered as a university economics lecturer, and his wife, Tita, also of regal Malay heritage. Tita was a prominent personality and commentator covering local cuisine at the Malay-speaking radio station. Their young daughter, Zeti, delighted Clifton and the Hendrickson children as they flew handmade kites in the Aziz's garden.

The Singapore and Malaysia academics graciously welcomed visiting faculty-with-families as if we were treasures on loan from renowned foreign institutions. I must not neglect the broader society of the Malaysian people, who were all generous in receiving us and most others, whom they simply designated as "European," a rubric that, at that time, included the handful of Americans.

Beyond our associations with the university people were others whose friendship we came to cherish. Charles Gamba was a highly regarded labor economist at the University of Malaya and Singapore's Labor Arbitration judge appointed by the new prime minister. His wife, Ina, was a glamorous, flamboyant personality whose caring and sensitivity for humankind were boundless, and whom I looked upon as a caring guardian.

A MATTER OF DIPLOMACY

Our friendship was such that I had no hesitation in approaching Ina as confidant concerning a little American/Singaporean matter of diplomatic delicacy that had surprisingly arisen. John D. Rockefeller 3rd's custom when traveling abroad was to pay a courtesy call on each foreign country's head of state. The indefinite delay by Singapore's new prime minister's office to receive Mr. Rockefeller created a bit of a stir among the Singapore business people—especially since the issue of Lee Kuan Yew's leftist leanings had not yet been clarified publicly.

To the shock of the Esso (the Rockefeller's Standard Oil, now Exxon) establishment, it was Clif who, among the big guys in the Singapore Rockefeller orbit, was able to make the announcement that the prime minister would be pleased to invite Mr. Rockefeller to his office for a meeting. How did this all come about? Briefly put: It was a private conversation between two very good friends, Ina Gamba and myself, that led to a behind-the-scenes action by Ina's husband, Charles. As a prominent member of Lee Kuan Yew's cabinet, Charles surreptitiously was, in this case of John D. Rockefeller 3rd, able to bypass the PM's refusal to receive any foreign visitors, thus eliminating an international stalemate.

We had countless vacation adventures with the Gambas, especially in Malacca, a one-time Portuguese port city that had become a most colorful tourist haven. Ina had discovered a former British colonial government rest house situated right on the beaches of the Straits of Malacca. We seemed to have access to the entire facility upon request, as the house was rarely visited by vacationers. Local legend held that there was a *hantu* (ghost) in residence in the house. It was understood that the ghost was quite harmless yet somewhat inconsiderate of sleeping

Treasured family friends Charles and Ina Gamba at our home in Kuala Lumpur, Malaysia (circa 1962)

Bruce and Clifton 3rd ready to be driven to their respective
British schools in Kuala Lumpur, Malaysia (1961)

Clifton 3rd and Bruce poking fun
at the photographer

guests. While we, of course, harbored no fears nor beliefs of any mysterious intruders, there was one occasion when Clif and an accompanying university dean both heard soft footsteps from a balcony for which there was no possible access other than through their respective bedrooms. We are pleased to offer this, our own supernatural occurrence, to the volumes of Malay *hantu* stories.

Clif's interaction with his Singapore university colleagues was essentially euphoric. Not surprisingly, there also were sticky exchanges related to economic ideologies, with occasional moments of sharp brinkmanship between Clif and the British school of Fabian socialist teaching. He was skillful in formal and informal arguments, sometimes engendering envy and resentment from his more-diehard teaching compatriots. My guess is that a bit of peer-envy was at issue here, especially given the high accolades voiced by so many of the students. Clif's academic prowess combined with his strong belief in himself had earned him considerable admiration from the young people.

His professional talent even surfaced impressively within the greater American community during a parent-teacher meeting at the Singapore American School where young Clifton was enrolled. Under discussion was the difficulty suffered by those students who had to alternate between grade schools overseas and in the United States. When families arrived back in Singapore following home leave, the youngsters invariably were placed in remedial classes. As passions and blame rose to a crescendo, Clif, standing tall among our American peers, stoically put the argument in perspective, saying that the so-called "remedial placement" was nothing more than a matter of correcting a lack of knowledge. "All education is correcting a lack of knowledge," he pointed out, and just because a particular student's deficiencies were greater than others, ascribing a pejorative label of "remedial" did not change the fact that the process was still education.

With incisive understanding of the subject and exquisite articulation, Clif was compelling in giving a simple explanation and clear path forward. Copious positive comments followed. Tom McHale, a parent and fellow economist, summed it up by saying, "Clif has always had the ability to speak on his feet." My husband's skill at expounding so effortlessly has countered many arguments throughout his career, enabling him to persuade and convince even his most rigid opponents.

MARTINIS AND FIREWORKS

While in Singapore, we were active members of the American Club, which included businessmen and women, diplomats, embassy staffers, and the smattering of academics from other American universities. Together we comprised a worthy sampling of American life in style, regional accents, popular music, you name it. One could see lots of stateside designer dresses to envy; A&W hot dogs and root beer were prominent; the bowling alley was a favorite playtime center; iced martinis were the favorite "sundowner"; and clever decorations were prominent in celebrating American holidays such as Halloween, Thanksgiving, and especially the Fourth of July.

For Independence Day in Kuala Lumpur we always visited the U.S. embassy residence, where the ambassador and his wife welcomed all American citizens to share in the celebrations. Everyone, especially the children, marveled at the grandiose fireworks displays. For me, the big lump-in-the throat, tears-in-the-eyes moment was seeing our U.S. Air Force planes soaring overhead in exquisite formation, dipping their wings in unison as a salute to us American citizens on the embassy grounds below, then spiraling off elegantly into the Asian skies.

At the Singapore American School young Clifton embraced his new life. He was a fun-loving child who made friends easily, but the multiple changes in our residences were discomforting for him. At three, he had attended a nursery school in Chicago, followed by a year at the Ethical Culture School in New York, and then he moved on to the Singapore American School. Two years later, he would attend the Alice Smith School in Kuala Lumpur, which was British in every sense of the word. Suddenly there was arithmetic taught in pounds, shillings, and pence, and British English spellings such as *colour* and *humour*. One impatient teacher, believing that the American children were being defiantly slow, repeatedly scolded Clifton and his young compatriots, taunting, "You Americans can do nothing but watch the telly!"

Despite Clifton's nimble sense of humor and ready wit, these multiple cultural differences required more adjustment than he believed was fair. He no sooner made buddies in one community than he had to bid them goodbye and start all over again in another setting. But he was well-equipped to dominate in the sport of "country name-dropping," sometimes annoying unsuspecting tourists with the revelation that young Clifton's travel portfolio far out-distanced their own.

The social stratification in both Singapore and Kuala Lumpur was structured to include the "number ones" of the diplomatic corps, corporations, foundations, and other key organizations—no matter how small. And we of the Council on Economic and Cultural Affairs were certainly small. Clif's position as lead-man in Singapore and Malaysia for CECA gave him the appropriate title such that our names were always included in the social A-list. Invitations to the many American, British, French, and German parties were prestigious and quite "proper" in form. Cocktail parties from seven to nine p.m. included the ambassadors or consuls general, CEOs of such firms as Esso and Kodak, and their wives. Dinner parties were always at eight p.m., with men dressed in lounge suits for dining—sport jackets were strictly for the golf course. Local European custom ordered after the final course following dessert, hostesses would invite the ladies to "powder our noses." Newcomers who declined to join the other ladies unknowingly committed a faux pas (while also missing out on the latest gossip). In neglecting the social rituals, the uninitiated would be subjected to subtle condescension by the veteran internationalists.

During the leave of the ladies, the gentlemen turned to cigars and brandy as the host casually invited one of his fellow guests to tell "a little" about his recent occupational interactions in the region. These occasions were actually drilling sessions, designed to demonstrate one's worth, professionally and intellectually. Fortunately for Clif, sparring with the intelligentsia was always his forte. Still, he was caught off guard the first time he found himself chosen for an interrogation by the other gents. Nonetheless, he acquitted himself admirably in his impromptu dissertation, notwithstanding the five-course meal, table wine, and brandy that preceded it.

THE ARTS COMMUNITY

My most engaging preoccupation during those years was stepping blithely into the burgeoning contemporary arts community. Visiting art galleries was totally natural for me, thanks to my exposure at the Little Red School House—that's simply what one does. I loved interacting with the young artists at their openings, inquiring about their inspirations, and quite often buying their works. I was the luckiest woman in the world to have arrived on this post-colonial scene just as Malaya was about to show the world its own national image, having been restrained subjects of the British Crown and its colonial culture for many decades. There were nationwide competitions of every sort: sports, gardening, poetry, music, and especially the painting, drawing, and sculpture. From my perspective, the visual artists were the most creative and productive.

There was an established set of senior professionals whose work was well regarded–and selling! Following Independence budding young enthusiasts practiced their artistry in several informally organized groups meeting around Kuala Lumpur. It was during the 1950s and 1960s that the nascent art scene actually blossomed as teachers and scholars with advanced degrees from the colleges and arts institutes in the U.S.A., England, Germany and France returned to Malaysia ushering in a new wave of skilled theoretical innovators. It was a fresh new era, and I was there to partake of it all.

Certainly other American patrons in residence coveted works of the recognized artists. The serious collectors would arrive promptly at the exhibition openings ready to get the first-crack at the installations of the superstars' (mostly the older artists) latest creations. Given the depth and range of my interest in the work of all of the artists, I was afforded a sincere welcome within their community. . . actually becoming recognized as an aficionado of the freshly burgeoning art scene. It was especially flattering when a curator from New York's Metropolitan Museum of Art sought my counsel when stopping over in Kuala Lumpur on a swing through the region. Flattered by such an inquiry and spurred on by Clif, I began writing my reactions to the burgeoning art scene, and eventually *Contemporary Artists of Malaysia: A Biographic Survey.*[3]

Published in 1971, my book was the first of its kind, presenting my interviews with twenty-seven leading artists, referencing their backgrounds, influences, and persuasions. On a hurried trip back to New York I carried a draft of the manuscript to share with several decision-making readers from the Asia Society, my publisher. One of the pundits advised, "Dolores, I want to see the faces of these multi-ethnic young people you write about!" As a result of that conversation, I routinely employed a local photographer to accompany me when making interviews. The photo images added to the readers' understanding of Malaysia's varied cultural differences. My study introduced a society of young talent that was energetic, passionate and not yet driven by commercialism. Rather, it was a burgeoning period of contemporary thought that was realistic and dedicated.

Once Malaysian art began to be recognized and valued, more money became available from the Malaysian government, local and multinational businesses based in Kuala Lumpur, international art colleges, foreign embassies, and other grant-making agencies. With bright young Malaysians returning from study abroad, the region's own motifs were utilized with more ingenuity than ever before. Some artists drew upon abstracted designs of the wood carvings on the bows of fishing boats, furious faces intended to frighten off evil sea demons. Others captured the figures of the Indonesian *wayang kulit*—leather puppets manipulated on sticks behind screens to produce huge images of the Ramayana characters in shadow plays.

The brilliantly colored Malay kites soaring and diving in the skies inspired reams of winsome designs among the younger adventurists. Still others drew ancient Jawi script, skillfully using its exotic lettering as subjects vital unto themselves. Most prominent were batiks, a method of designing cotton cloth through multiple dyeings and waxings, usually used for sarongs worn by both women and men. Though the craft was original to Indonesia, it was Chuah Thean Teng from Penang, Malaysia, who turned the process into a medium for creating fine art. And essential to the artistic language was the use of Chinese ink and wash on rice paper.

3 Published for the Asia Society, NY, by the Union Cultural Organization Sdn. Bhd. Selangor, Malaysia, 1971.

Montage of Malaysian artists' paintings from my book, *Contemporary Artists of Malaysia*

Abdul Latiff, *Lahuma II* – ink on paper etching (No 3), 1969

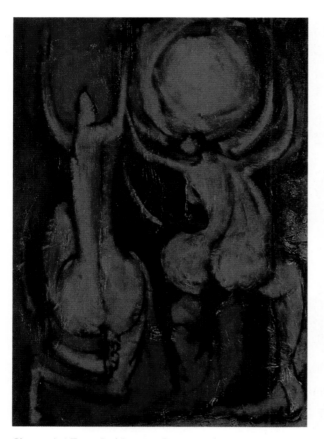

Cheong Lai Tong, *Red Dancing Figures* – oil on canvas, 1962

Cheong Soo Pieng, *Malay Fishing Village* – ink and colors on paper, n.d.

Chuah Thean Teng, *Crab Catcher* – Batik on cloth, 1960s

Dzulkifli Buyong, *Muslims At Prayer* – pastel on paper, 1962

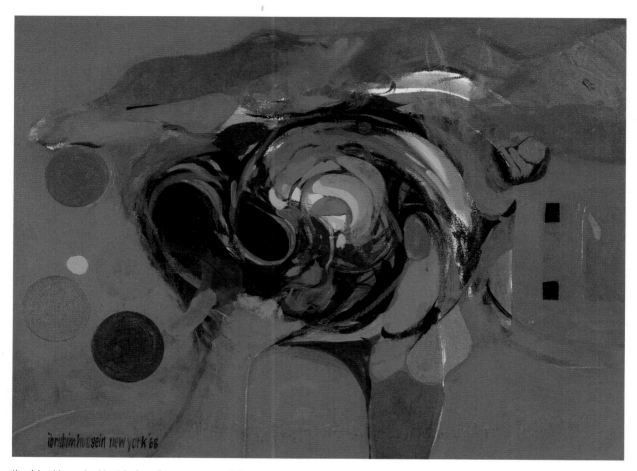

Ibrahim Hussein, Untitled – oil on canvas, 1966

Jolly Koh, Untitled – watercolor on paper, 1971

Lee Joo For, *Oriental Talisman* – etching (No. 4), 1966

Syed Ahmad Jamal, *Rockin'*– acrylic on canvas, 1969

Yeoh Jinleng, *Dance of the Gopis with Lord Krishna* - charcoal drawing, 2012

Daring to generalize, I found the colors of the Malaysians were drawn from their varying ethnic preferences, such as the garden pastel blues and yellows of the Malays, the swirling hot-spice oranges and pinks of the Indians, and the aggressive reds and golds of the Chinese. This blending and wide variety of creations offered a distinctively Malaysian flavor. Most meaningful, I believe the arts developed less out of a need to produce income than a desire for individual and national expression.

Eventually my book was recognized within the annals of Malaysian art history. Forty-five years following its publication it was reviewed by Dr. Emelia Ong Ian Li, a Malaysian arts scholar who credited my work as an important source in discovering the beginning of the contemporary arts of Malaysia.

"In the organization of the book," she wrote, *"her authorial voice is revealed in the way she contextualizes the artists within the narrative of identity formation in the newly independent Malaysia. In this sense, she contends that art should also be understood beyond the personal histories of the artists...Even though the book provides an overview rather than a comprehensive description of the Malaysian art scene, Wharton's inclusion of factual details is sufficient to make it a useful source of information, both for the casual reader as well as the art historian...The book became a resource for subsequent art writers and art historians who refer to the artists' interviews as a record of their candid responses to the exciting period that was the 1950s and 1960s. Their responses were also thoughtful statements about art itself and reveal highly personal reflections on Malaysian art that remain relevant today."*[4]

Following independence, arts activities expanded, ushering in a number of signature cultural events for which I was called to participate. One such invitation was to serve with several established local artists as judge for the First National Children's Art Competition. The well-publicized event was the brainchild of Datin (a title of eminence) Uma Sambanthan, whose husband, Dato V.T. Sambanthan (Minister of Works, Posts and Telecommunications) had founded the Malayan Times national newspaper. Minister Sambanthan was leader of the Malayan Indian Congress, and Uma was his deeply respected wife and constant companion.

---

4 Emelia Ong Ian Li, "Book Review: *Contemporary Artists of Malaysia: A Biographic Survey*," in *Narratives in Malaysian Art: Perspectives*, Volume IV, Soon, Simon et al., Rogue Art, Kuala Lumpur, December 2017.

Our panel agreed unanimously to award first prize to "Muslims at Prayer" a tenderly religious pastel by teenage Dzulkifli Buyong. Uma Sambanthan paid me the great honor of giving *Muslims At Prayer* to me. Recognizing the painting's historic value, I believed it should be guaranteed professional conservators' protective care. Now, this iconic treasure resides in the permanent collection at the Johnson Museum of Cornell University, part of a gift of fifteen paintings that Clif and I donated to that school. Uma Sambanthan, now retired, remains a steadfast advocate and promoter of children's art, and it is with the deepest gratitude that our friendship continues to this day.

Then there was a double-header invitation to serve with some fellow Americans on a committee to participate in a Malaysian cause—our host country's desire for a National Monument to honor its military, which had struggled for freedom during the Japanese Occupation of World War II as well as the Malayan Emergency and the Japanese occupation 1948–1960. The commemorative trophy was based on the Iwo Jima sculpture created by Felix de Weldon for the Marine Corps War Memorial. During a visit to Washington, DC, Malaysia's Prime Minister, Tunku Abdul Rahman, had seen the large bronze work and inquired about having a similar piece recognizing his country's war heroes.

We Americans responded by establishing a fund-raising initiative, the National Monument Fund. The working committee was organized by Bill Fleming, the Asia Foundation's representative in Malaysia. I worked diligently with Betty Chen, descendant of one of Singapore's most distinguished families, and other socially active Americans to raise public resources worthy of an honorable salute to Malaysia and the Prime Minister, whom we warmly called, "Bapa Malaysia" (Father of Malaysia).

Then in August 1963 I was asked to serve as a judge to help choose decorative panels for the new Parliament House in Kuala Lumpur, which I accepted with enormous pride.

But most surprising was a request from the University of Malaya's student association, the Persekutuan Bahasa Melayu (Malay Language Society), to choreograph several original dances for them to present on campus in 1962 and 1963. I created two compositions based on local games and a third drawn from the shadow puppets of the epic Ramayana plays. Of the latter, lead dancer Marina Merican Samad reminisced in her blog *The Reluctant Raconteur*: "Dolores cleverly blended modern dance techniques with those of traditional Malay dance. In our first dance we

Uma Sambanthan, adored friend and supporter, holding daughter Kunjari, Kuala Lumpur, Malaysia (circa 1963)

formed rows which crisscrossed each other many times at different angles, the girls gracefully waving scarves in time to traditional Malay music. The second was a stylized football game played by the boys with the girls as ardent spectators. The third was a 'wayang kulit' or shadow play based on the Ramayana Hindu Epic. I was thrilled to be chosen to dance the part of Princess Sita. During her husband's absence, Sita is abducted by the demon god Ravana but her husband eventually rescues her with the help of Hanuman, the monkey god. We wore elaborate costumes and moved in small steps, puppet-like, behind a giant lighted screen, like a real shadow play, but from time to time emerged to dance in front of it."

With full collaboration—even more accurately said, enthusiastic participation—of the students, we staged a memorable production. In designing the costumes for the dances set in present-day vistas, we borrowed from their traditional Malay dress: *baju kebaya dan kein* (blouses with wrist-length sleeves and wraparound long skirts) for the girls, and

Malay students for whom
I choreographed two original
dance dramas given in recital
at the University of Malaya

baju sampan dan singkat (handsome hip-covering sashes over conventional shirts and slacks topped off with the songkok, Malay black hat) for the boys.

The most dramatic costuming was the headdresses for the three characters in the Ramayana play that were truly artistic treasures. When discussing the wardrobe with the students I had remarked wistfully, "Wish we could get Nik Zainal Abidin to design the gold crown for Princess Sita and the masks for our Prince Rama and the Hanuman." I knew the artist for his greatly admired sketches of mythical animal figures. Furthermore, I had interviewed him for my book. One of the student dancers modestly interjected, "I know Nik pretty well. I'll ask him." And he did! Much to the delight of us all, the headdresses turned out to be of museum quality. (We did return the masks to Nik following the performances.) When all pulled together, the production was received with high applause.

Marina Merican in the role of Princess Sita Devi is guided by the Hanuman wearing headdress and mask designed by artist Nik Zainal Abidin.

In retrospect, choreographing for the students offered me a double exposure to Malayan culture. First was the unique opportunity for a deeper, more active involvement with the young people, and second was in being the agent to invoke a new aesthetic.

An article in the *Malayan Times* proclaimed that the performances displayed "dynamism, movement, colour, and excellent choreography." However, there was one devastating moment after I allowed a reporter and photographer from another paper, *The Straits Times,* to observe a rehearsal. Good publicity, I thought. Alas, the photographer stood just below the stage and shot upward so the girls' legs were prominently visible. The next day's paper bore the headline, "Not Quite the Same as Grandpa's Time," showing swirling skirts swinging well above the ankle. I was mortified. After all, these were Islamic university students who had invited me to introduce a new artistic expression—not to offend their very strict religious codes.

Needing some consoling, I made a "trunk call" to Clif, who was on a field trip in Bangkok. He said, "Come here to me! The *amahs* can take care of the boys for a few days. You need a break!"

His sweet embrace assuaged my crushed spirits, as did a follow-up article by my friend, Uma Sambanthan, with a write-up in the *Malayan Times* saying, "'Malam Irama' is an Imaginative Show." The pain of *The Straits Times* story was thus short-lived, and complimentary remarks did

As a trustee of the Asia Society, I met with many diplomats. Here, I chat with Adam Malik, right, ambassador and future vice president of Indonesia, and Kenneth Young, Asia Society president and former U.S. ambassador to Thailand. (October 1969)

finally abound. Most gratifying was the reaction from the students, who were sad that their request for a modern Malaysian dance had been accomplished but was now past. "No more choreography!" they lamented.

As our six years' residency in Southeast Asia came to an end and we prepared to depart, I mused over how my daily activities and aesthetic proclivities had been enriched. Happily, there were many return visits with Clif, as well as corporate travel abroad as part of my directorships for Phillips Petroleum and the Gannett media company. Returning to those deeply familiar sites was poignant, as I wanted to snatch back those days and to remain involved. Even to this day, I feel an abiding joy simply in recalling all I experienced. There had been an acceptance of beauty beyond my own culture, an understanding of the grace and aggravations of different gods, a recognition of the abundance of nature's marvels—fruits, animals, sun, and sea—and to believing in the possibilities of new horizons and other galaxies.

CHAPTER 6

Michigan State University

When Clif was appointed president of Michigan State University, the story made national news. The October 18, 1969 *New York Times* placed the announcement "above the fold" (top of the front page) under the headline: "Negro Economist Is Named Head of Michigan State U." At a social gathering that evening, I ran into the *NYT*'s celebrated columnist Seymour Topping, whom we had met in Kuala Lumpur. Grabbing my arm, Top (as he was known to his colleagues) pressed hurriedly, "Where is Clif? He is the man of the hour!"

My husband had shaken up the status quo, having been chosen to lead MSU, making him the second Black to head a predominately white institution of higher education, and the first since 1874, when Patrick Francis Healy, a mulatto, became president of Georgetown University. Now Clif would take command of one of America's major research universities. His place in academic history was established.

The news-making appointment was not a surprise to our close professional friends. After our return to the United States, Clif had become a hot property, frequently approached for prominent leadership positions. His increased visibility was due, in part, to his role in running the ADC's American Universities Research Program, which involved directing seminars and workshops and making grants to faculty inexperienced at research in the developing world. These foundation activities became a showcase for Clif's talents, as he spearheaded initiatives that involved hundreds of administrators of major universities across the country. Furthermore, he was invited to serve on the State Department's East Asia and Pacific Advisory Committee, and he was sought out by prestigious boards like the Asia Society and the Overseas Development

"Ourselves" at home in our New York city apartment before taking up reins at MSU.

Council. Nelson Rockefeller asked him to join his Presidential Mission to Latin America commissioned by Richard Nixon.

When the University of Michigan included Clif on *its* short list for president, it became apparent that a change in his career path was inevitable. Then along came MSU, known for being among the earliest land-grant universities.

Several days before the announcement, and before we knew whether or not Clif would be awarded the presidency, we met with the MSU trustees. The mood of the eight men shuffling about in the drab midtown Manhattan hotel room was somewhat dull. I was at ease with trustee Stephen Nisbet's probing interview. It soon became apparent that the backdrop of our conversation was to better understand what I, as MSU's First Lady, would or would not have to offer in that prestigious and quite visible role. Trustee Blanche Martin, a Black former football star and zealous MSU alumnus, lightened the tension when he accidentally brushed against a bucket of ice cubes, which crackled noisily as they splattered on the graying carpet, leading him to jest, "Wow, what was in those cubes?"

Don Stevens and Warren Huff appeared to butt heads over the process of the presidential selection, while other trustees sat motionless in their straight-back chairs, brows squinting at Nisbet and me as we cheerfully rated the current Broadway shows, art museums, favorite restaurants, and life in Asia and our sons. The hour with the trustees concluded, Clif and I popped into a taxi and rushed back to our 88th Street apartment and our two boys.

"How do you think the meeting went?" I asked with a hint of trepidation.

Clif's response was exactly what I needed to hear: "Whatever their reaction, I think it went just fine!"

Clif's MSU appointment was followed by a deluge of phone calls, telegrams, and scores of letters requesting interviews or sending congratulations from all over the country and as far away as Singapore and Kuala Lumpur.

For me the earth shook more than a little. I had felt myself a part of the ADC, the John D. Rockefeller 3rd organization that had opened the exotic world of Southeast Asia to us. Furthermore, having benefitted personally and professionally by writing my as-yet-unpublished *Contemporary Artists of Malaysia*, I had thoughts of traveling in the region and writing about other contemporary Asian arts for an interested American public. Now I was about to enter the world of a university's First Lady. This was going to force an enormous shift away from previous ambitions. I was dismayed by the challenge facing me–but intrigued by the prospect of a new adventure.

Our lives, already directed on a fascinating course in pursuit of discovery and fulfillment, began a very different journey when our plane landed at the Lansing, Michigan, airport on November 1, 1969, at the start of homecoming weekend for the alumni of MSU. While Clif had visited the campus many times before, holding ADC conferences associated with the College of Agriculture, this was my first step into a Midwestern state I was being asked to call home. Fellow travelers strained to see who among the disembarking passengers was attracting all the attention as a large contingent of photographers hoisted their cameras, reporters pulled microphones from their cases, and university officials scurried behind the portable stairs being positioned alongside the aircraft. Suddenly the spotlight was on us.

After descending the stairs, Clif stood tall and composed as he respectfully extended his hand to Walter Adams, an economics professor of considerable popularity who would continue to serve as acting president until Clif officially took office on January 2. Adams's persona was the opposite of Clif's. Students found Adams an uproarious character with his dangling cigar, high-stepping stride (typically clowning

Clif and I walk out on the Spartan Stadium field to cheers for MSU's newly instated First Family. (Nov. 1, 1969)

in front of MSU's Spartan Marching Band), and ever-present barrel of wisecracks to please the crowd. Adams exuberantly greeted Clif as the cameras whirled, catching his fervent welcome for MSU's new leader. Or was this effusive "hail to the chief" actually a cover for his own candidacy having been rejected?

ON THE FIFTY-YARD LINE

That Saturday afternoon was my introduction to Big Ten football. During my college dating years, I had attended the Harvard/Yale and Army/Navy games; I'd even spent time in high school as a cheerleader. Big Ten football presented a totally different experience. The two and a half hours spent in the president's box watching the MSU vs. Indiana game was mesmerizing—especially thanks to the outrageously dressed fans roaring in resounding waves of song, "Go Green and Go White! Go! Go! Go!"

My excitement skyrocketed when Clif and I walked out to the fifty-yard line of Spartan Stadium and 77,500 football people stood to cheer the new First Couple of MSU. I haven't gotten over that moment yet! Ten-year-old

Bruce, who had accompanied us as far as the sidelines, said afterward, "Mom, I've never seen you smile like that before!" I was on the verge of tearing up.

Next on the schedule was a meeting with Joy Adcock, the university's chief of decorating, who would escort me through our new home, Cowles House. As I stepped into the formal entryway, she slipped off her glove and extended her right hand in a most courteous and deferential welcome. Joy was the epitome of professionalism, radiating a generosity of intent to be of service to me as the university's First Lady and mistress of Cowles House. She, a seasoned decorator, and I, the patron, just clicked in our relationship as we walked through the various sections of the residence. There were rooms for entertaining and family living, numerous service areas, and an apartment for a live-in housekeeper. There were a walk-in freezer and an even larger cold room for storing meat—the former president, John Hannah, ran a farm with many head of cattle for butchering.

In the middle of the walk-through, Bruce upstaged Mrs. Adcock by announcing that he had already counted nine bathrooms. Every turn of

Cowles House, the official campus residence of the MSU president, where we lived for eight years

I lead the Pledge of Allegiance before 77,500 football fans at Spartan Stadium during the MSU vs. Wisconsin game. Beside me is Ken Bloomquist, director, MSU Marching Band. (Nov. 3, 1973)

the head revealed fine appointments, beautiful wood paneling, exquisite fabrics and carpeting. Given the dignity the Hannahs had infused in the entertaining areas of the house, I believed that the more classic European service that I had practiced throughout our years living abroad in Singapore, Malaysia, and the diplomatic world would be most appropriate in Cowles House.

I was seduced by the serene nobility of the place. Foreign travel with Clif on his official assignments had exposed me to a number of embassy residences, and I was elated to find this MSU presidential manor house equal to the finest of them.

During our first days in residence at Cowles House, the doorbells of the three entrances seemed to ring constantly, announcing deliveries of welcoming gifts: bouquets of poinsettias, roses, and amaryllis, boxes of giant red apples, and carefully preserved Michigan cherries. Then, finally, the moving van arrived from New York City bearing our personal effects. Just as the men began unloading our furniture, garment bags, and tons of book boxes, a local television crew pulled into the side entrance.

"Mrs. Wharton! Mrs. Wharton!" Virginia Blair, our housekeeper, announced in a hurried voice, "There are some reporters and cameramen asking to talk with you. They say they want to film your moving in!"

I hesitated briefly and greeted the newsmen with a smile calculated to disarm as I said, half-apologetically, "I feel like a lady unexpectedly caught in public view with curlers in her hair. Please allow me to extend an invitation to you when we are settled." The more the reporters insisted, the more I smiled while firmly establishing my resistance with the promise of an open door in the future. They didn't return anytime soon—at least not until other, bigger issues were in play.

Though I felt a tinge of annoyance at the intrusion, it was quickly replaced with a sense of victory at having successfully dealt with what could have resulted in a most unflattering story—a possible *Putney Swope*[1] headline about a Black couple taking over the esteemed MSU manor house. Assuredly, there were other imbroglios ahead with the press.

The aggravation was quickly forgotten, as several giggling coeds appeared at the front entrance and pointed cheerfully to their dormitory, Landon Hall, directly opposite Cowles House. A huge banner stretched some thirty feet across the front of the dorm, reading, "Dear Whartons, Welcome to MSU!" Clif and I were captivated by this affectionate greeting from our nearest neighbors. That welcome, along with countless others from students all over the campus who spontaneously expressed their delight over Clif's appointment, elevated our spirits to greater heights.

Our arrival at Michigan State was not all bouquets and applause; there were some treacherous players behind the scenes who bore watching. Three trustees who had voted against Clif's election soon proved to be a wicked lobby. It had been well-known that Warren Huff had wanted G. Mennen "Soapy" Williams, Michigan's former governor, to be named MSU's president, as did his fellow trustees Clare White and Frank Hartman.

At a reception given in our honor by Walter Adams, for some fifty prominent friends of the university, I suddenly became aware of Bruce's absence. He was quite a sociable lad, accustomed to chatting up guests at our homes in Kuala Lumpur and New York City, so I wouldn't expect him to shy away from the crowd. Clif and I began a quiet search throughout

---

1 *Putney Swope* is a 1969 movie comedy about a Black man who is inadvertently elected chairman of a company's board of directors and the humorous havoc that ensues.

the main floor. Finally, it occurred to us to look in the basement, though it wasn't set up for entertainment. To my amazement, there we found the trio of scoundrels—Huff, Hartman, and White—grilling Bruce about our family lifestyle and intimate relationship. I was outraged that our young son was being pumped in an effort to uncover some dark side of our lives that they might use against Clif. After that, we limited Bruce's participation in large university events in the residence, at least those including the trustees.

There were other less-cunning but equally crude attempts to pry into our personal lives. Several days after Bruce started fifth grade at Central Elementary School in East Lansing, the principal called to ask if I had given permission for a newspaper reporter and photographer to follow our son during his first couple of days in the school. A *State Journal* reporter had simply walked into the classrooms to observe Bruce and how his classmates might accept or reject him. I was aghast to think that our adored ten-year-old son's first hours with his new classmates would be exploited so diabolically. I will be ever grateful to that wise and caring principal who, after speaking with me, promptly showed the reporter the exit.

THE AGE OF PROTESTS

Six weeks later Clifton 3rd paid his first weekend visit to Michigan State. As a seventeen-year-old high school senior, with only five months until graduation from the Dalton School, he had remained in New York City, living at the home of a classmate. I had his name paged on the loudspeaker as soon as his plane landed at the Lansing airport, and when he came to the phone I apologized for not being on hand to greet him, explaining that several hundred students were rioting on campus. Throughout East Lansing, the students were protesting the conviction of the Chicago Seven, leaders of the anti-war demonstrations during the 1968 Democratic Convention in Chicago. The violent confrontations between protesters and police were widely televised and had shocked the nation. The leaders had been tried and found guilty, provoking an escalation in demonstrations on many college campuses across the U.S.

I asked young Clifton to take a taxi. I was reluctant to leave Cowles House unattended, since it had for years been a focal point for students protesting the war. His cabdriver stopped at the edge of the campus, saying that he could not drive farther due to the student disturbances.

On departing the taxi, Clifton 3rd approached a campus policeman and asked for directions to Cowles House. The officer requested identification, explaining that non-students were not allowed to enter the university grounds because of the unrest. As a follow-up question the officer asked our son to identify himself.

"I'm Clifton Wharton!" said our son, a long-haired, six-foot-four teenager, wearing blue jeans and a denim jacket on which he had sewn a badge proving his participation in the recent Moratorium March on Washington.

The campus officer retorted slowly in a measured tone, "Yeaaah, right!"

To wit, young Clifton arrived at the front door of our new residence with police escort. I held my head in disbelief and mused, *What have we gotten our dear little family into?*

Later that same evening, Dick Bernitt, the head of MSU's Department of Public Safety, came to our home to update my husband about the growing demonstrations on Grand River Avenue, with protesters now numbering some five hundred or possibly even more students. The activists wanted to add their outrage to the anger being expressed across the nation, leading to major uprisings in East Lansing and on the campus. Clif concluded that it was best to disabuse the ringleaders from thinking they might be successful in building a common rage and possibly

Clif's first student demonstration and me at his side, on the steps of the Student Union building (Feb. 19, 1970).

We are joined by son Clifton 3rd.

In full riot gear, the Lansing police prepare to confront student protestors on Grand River Avenue, February 19, 1970.

expanding their numbers. Leaving Bruce in Cowles House in the care of a security officer, and accompanied by a half dozen other officers, Clif, Clifton 3rd, and I walked over to the Student Union building, where we were greeted by a noisy and jeering crowd. With bullhorn in hand, Clif confronted perhaps two hundred demonstrators and, in a firm, sober voice, asked for calm—the first of many such occasions to follow.

Suddenly, Dick Bernitt asked, "Where is your son?"

Where indeed! Clifton 3rd was standing among the protesters, watching events unfold. Once Clifton 3rd was spotted, Bernitt covertly moved through the crowd, calmly taking our son in tow, leading him back to stand beside his dad and me. In reminiscing years later about the event, Clifton 3rd said that the experience was one of the most disconcerting of his life. Sympathizing with the protesters, yet standing with his parents, who represented the power elite, he felt his identity and sense of self had been severely challenged.

That evening was an initiation for all of us. In his first confrontation with the activists, Clif clearly demonstrated that he was resolute in standing firm, vocal, and unruffled. Thereafter, students referred to him as "Mr. Cool." Clif's order to keep the University open prevailed. As for Clifton 3rd's reaction to the weekend, he looked around at his new home and commented mockingly, "Hmm, nice place to visit."

Whether we fancied our new lifestyle or not, we found ourselves catapulted into the arena of Michigan luminaries. No doubt our high profile was largely due to Clif's position as president, but I believe it also was attributable to curiosity about a young Black family redefining racial perceptions in America. Clif's and my prominence escalated dramatically. Wherever we went, there seemed to be photographers documenting our every move and comment. To a certain extent, it was exciting, but when the glare failed to diminish, it became wearing.

Michiganders are driven by a combination of self-assurance and curiosity. When they sought my participation in community arts projects, I returned their inquiries with genuine enthusiasm. Our shared teamwork became exceptionally productive. I developed treasured lifelong friendships. High on that list were puppeteer Phyllis Maner and her husband, Bud, an accountant, both MSU grads who were strong community arts advocates.

We also bonded with Jim Bonnen, one of Clif's stalwart faculty supporters, and his wife, Sally, the family center, a role for which she sweetly downplayed her own scholarly achievements, culminating with a PhD in literature. Both wives served independently as team players. There were *State Journal* publisher Louis Weil, actor and arts activist Evie Machtel, the Stoddards, the Seamans, and other spirited Michiganders with whom we shared common interests and holiday celebrations. With such a supportive base of caring friends, the spotlight ceased to be a concern, and I became quite at ease in my role as MSU's First Lady. However, throughout my eight years in that auspicious role, I faithfully wished upon the evening star that I might play my part as best as providence in all its magical powers would permit.

Given the vastness of the university, with its diversity of organizations, associations, and clubs, along with our outreach into

"RECEPTIONS! RECEPTIONS! RECEPTIONS!" We welcomed over 5,000 guests annually in addition to the most honored of all—our students.

multiple social, business, academic, and cultural sectors of Michigan in the name of the university, our popularity increased considerably, requiring daily scheduling by the hour. Much to my amazement, the excitement that began on our arrival never abated—rather it grew exponentially as the years progressed.

FACULTY FOLK

Shortly after Clif's appointment as president and before leaving New York City, I received a letter from the president of the Faculty Folk—a prominent, long-established group comprising the wives of faculty, administrators, researchers, and more. The club's president requested that "the Faculty Folk's first meeting of the New Year be held in Cowles House." I was thrilled at the prospect of greeting the faculty wives and responded accordingly.

Soon after we arrived on campus, she called and asked when we might meet in Cowles House to discuss the arrangements for the upcoming reception. My past practice as a member of the University of Chicago Dames Club led me to expect a copy of the invitation and the number of guests expected to attend, with remaining details to be left to me. But to my surprise, a follow-up telephone conversation revealed that the club president had envisioned herself presiding over the entire event in my home. In this little incident, I quickly learned an important lesson: Watch out for presumptive visionary volunteers with designs on assuming my role.

A fortuitous coincidence allowed me to gracefully retract my invitation. Though Cowles House is the president's private home, it is very much a university-maintained facility. In fact, the residence, including the kitchen, was locked into the campus-wide maintenance schedule for regular servicing and repairs, which on this occasion conveniently overlapped with the timing for the Faculty Folk reception. I had no recourse but to send my regrets, saying that we could not hold the event in Cowles House but I would instead honor my commitment to Faculty Folk at the superbly qualified Kellogg Hotel and Conference Center. Not surprisingly, I received cool stares of indignation from the club president throughout the reception.

As a result of this incident, I decided that Cowles House would remain committed to receiving students, alumni, and donors, but beyond that, our receptions would be limited to welcoming high-profile guests of the university. I am delighted to say that an invitation to the residence from Clif and me was welcomed as a prestigious gesture throughout our tenure and beyond.

Over the years, I was invited to join numerous clubs and organizations in the community, all of which I gracefully declined. Wanting to be available to all interest groups benefitting the university and to maintain comparable relationships with them, I decided to commit myself to specific events as they arose, rather than joining their ranks as a participating member.

ART AT COWLES HOUSE

In that I was the enlightened daughter-in-law of Ambassador Wharton, and with a first-hand understanding of proper social protocol, I made courtesy calls soon after arriving in Michigan to three individuals out of recognition and respect for their leadership. The first was a visit with Sarah Hannah, who had reigned most graciously as First Lady of Michigan State University for twenty-eight years and also was the daughter of President Emeritus Robert S. Shaw. My second call was upon Helen Milliken, founder of the extraordinary national arts initiative Artrain and, most significantly, wife of the governor of Michigan. Both women and their husbands were generous in their support and consideration of Clif and me. My third call was to Professor Erling Brauner, the distinguished chairman of MSU's Art Department. In adapting to new locations, I had always found it valuable to explore events within the local arts arena, and with the professors' assistance, I hoped to do the same at Michigan State.

Professor Brauner, a veteran guiding the department through a number of penurious years, graciously seated me beside his very neat desk in his unpretentious office, his wiry white eyebrows arching with unsuppressed curiosity over my intentions. A graduate of Cornell, he was typically old-school Ivy League, accustomed to bowing to ladies in social settings but, at this moment, puzzled by a visit from the wife of the university's chief executive, he sat with his back firmly upright. Following Erling Brauner's cordial welcome, he asked if I'd like to tour the department, to which I responded with an enthusiastic, "But of course!"

His was an invitation that opened the doors to what became a bountiful universe of kindred souls. The professor and I strolled into classrooms, through studios, labs, and workshops; he gave me facts, figures, comparison ratios for faculty and students, course descriptions, and answers to all of my seriously intended questions. We stopped frequently to chat with the teaching staff, while the students toting canvases, easels, and mountainous paraphernalia were too absorbed in each other to notice the chairman and his guest. In passing along the corridors, the ever-garrulous professors respectfully acknowledged their leader but turned their heads with a quick backward glance to scrutinize his companion. We concluded the walk-round in the basement, where several kilns were at-the-ready, awaiting quantities of freshly designed crockery.

The university had a well-established arts program with many studio professors engaged in teaching and showing their work off-campus apart from the Lansing area. Most any MSU administrator would shamelessly admit that the Art Department received far less recognition than the university's coddled athletes, given the long-standing passion for football and basketball by the alumni and other sports enthusiasts. It was no surprise that my request to pay a courtesy call on the chairman of the Art Department was met with apathetic interest by Clif's administrative advisors as "a harmless visit for the First Lady to make."

During my conversation with Professor Brauner, I mentioned my desire to provide the studio art faculty a prominent showcase in the public spaces of Cowles House. Clif and I hosted events there for some four thousand graduating students, and counting our other guests, we received more than five thousand people annually. Having been active in the Museum of Modern Art's Junior Council and its Art Lending Service, I had two years' experience working in a highly active art-rental program. I visited midtown Manhattan galleries to identify pieces appropriate for loaning to the membership, and a MoMA curator, Campbell Wyly, made the final selection that went into the groups to be rented. (My services always were pro bono and I never received financial compensation for this work.)

Once the Art at Cowles House project got under way, professors would bring their work to a room in the Art Department, where Erling Brauner and I met alone to make the selections. The studio art faculty honored me richly. Most of them were showing in private galleries in New York, Chicago, Grand Rapids, and Detroit. They worked in oils, acrylics, canvas, metals, clay, plaster, wood, and all things imaginable (not to mention some media that were decidedly *not* imaginable). I was elated that they trusted me with a part of themselves that was so personally and professionally precious.

First faculty art collection arrives at Cowles House with Brauner and me at-the-ready to install.

We changed the artwork on a quarterly calendar. The schedule was my own to keep, but the expectation by the public proved to be quite keen, leading many to ask, "So, what's next?" The program opened doors leading me to a romance with the studio art academics, the greater university, the East Lansing community, and well beyond.

Art at Cowles House received a terrific splash when it was featured by Jeanne Whittaker, a columnist for the *Detroit Free Press*. This welcoming salute by a major urban paper led smaller local papers to follow suit. Consequently, my program received a lot of press throughout Mid Michigan.

My initial meeting with Jeanne Whittaker was at her initiative, a story that goes back to that early period when I was avoiding all media people with a vengeance. During one of my first interviews, a young female columnist with the *Lansing State Journal* asked what I thought of graffiti, a new public phenomenon that was often crude and sometimes profane and blasphemous. Considering myself a broad-minded arts advocate, I

I welcome a sweeping range
of community visitors to see
Art in Cowles House

Detroit Free Press article by Jeanne Whittaker that raised my profile throughout Michigan as an arts advocate (March 8, 1970)

responded, "Graffiti has not yet matured, nor has it been well-defined, but it is a genre that should be watched." Next day, my comment had been twisted to read, "The New President's Wife Loves Graffiti." I was aghast and vowed never to speak with any reporters again.

Thus, when Jeanne chased me down at a reception and called out, "I won't hurt you!" I wanted to run and hide. But that was not possible in this mansion filled with Michigan establishment who had been invited to meet Clif and me. Finally I stopped and hesitantly chatted with the *Detroit Free Press* columnist. She asked if she might visit me in Cowles

House for an interview. I was skeptical but agreed. From that interview on, my life in the public eye was altered. The power of the press is enormous, and thereafter its force became typically positive in my favor in Michigan.

MY ART WORLD EXPANDING

One of a small group of high priestesses ruling the Detroit Institute of Arts was Lydia Winston Malbin, whose golden lineage and personal commitment gave her a dominant seat among the arts leadership of old Detroit. Daughter of the famed industrial architect Albert Kahn, she had grown up surrounded by original works of Courbet, Manet, Monet, and Utrillo. But she became independently respected for her landmark collection of Futurist painters.

Conversation with Lydia was free-flowing given my familiarity with the New York art scene and my involvement at MoMA. In addition, my soon-to-be-published book about the contemporary artists of Malaysia prompted even more chatty exchanges.

Prior to leaving New York, I had spoken in public forums about my research on Malaysian art. Also, the University of Michigan and Miami University in Ohio had hosted me for television presentations. Donna Stein, a prints scholar on staff at MoMA and commentator of a television series on contemporary art, interviewed me for one of her shows, which was rebroadcast by a Michigan TV station.

Such was the basis for an invitation to appear as a guest speaker at a patrons' membership luncheon in the Detroit Institute of Art's indoor garden. I prepared a comprehensive slide presentation of Malaysian artists and their work that gave me a substantive introduction to the DIA membership. Over time, a most cordial relationship developed between the DIA and me, and eventually I joined the institute's Board of Trustees.

Additional attractive invitations followed. Governor Milliken appointed me to his Michigan Special Committee on Architecture and to the Michigan Council of the Arts. I had a semi-political appointment as co-chair beside Lieutenant Governor James Brickley in presiding over Michigan's role in the United States Bicentennial celebration. In addition, John D. Rockefeller 3rd asked me to join his National Committee on the Bicentennial as a trustee. After I accepted, "Mr. John" grinned broadly and declared, "*Now* you are a member of the Establishment!"

My inauguration as
Vice Chair of the Michigan
Bicentennial

THE NATIONAL ENDOWMENT FOR THE ARTS

I will advance momentarily to 1974, when I was appointed by President
Gerald Ford as a council member for the National Endowment for the
Arts. The NEA was still in its infancy, with the critical mission to nur-
ture, inspire, and share the magnificent wealth of the many cultural pil-
lars created within the United States. The role of the council members
was to advise the NEA chairman by voicing our opinions, criticisms, and
ideas during quarterly three-day meetings.

The NEA chairmen during my years were Nancy Hanks (with Vice
Chair Michael Straight occasionally assuming leadership when Nancy
was on leave), then Livingston Biddle and, by the end of my term, Frank
Hodsoll. The atmosphere in the agency was fostered by the unique dynamism inherent in a brand-new body struggling for its very existence.
The drive against acceptance of the NEA by an often-spiteful Congress
inspired the crusading staff with ever-greater determination.

I was excited by the opportunity to become acquainted with the multiple art forms from around the country. This experience was a big-screen
continuation of my earlier studies of Asian arts. Council members were
required to read hundreds of proposals from established institutions such
as the Metropolitan Museum of Art and the New York Philharmonic, as

well as numerous regional groups, all seeking funds from the designated arts disciplines—dance, literature, media arts, visual arts, music, opera, theater, and more. Though the Endowment's funding from Congress was grudgingly small, inherent in the awards was an official imprimatur that each grantee could use as a powerful tool for raising additional funds.

I was honored when Nancy Hanks asked me to navigate a proposal called the Million Dollar Match through the proceedings required for a newly created program. The recommendation to the council for its approval was heavily debated in open public debates. Seated in the meeting hall—usually the ballroom of a major Washington hotel—were staff from all disciplines, panelists, arts advocates, foundation executives, even congressmen such as John Brademas. The debate focused on whether a million dollars should be spent on another initiative rather than spreading the money among existing programs in dire need—even though the benefits of the Million Dollar Match was intended to challenge the private sector to anti-up with new monies. After passionate pleas on both sides, the Million Dollar Match won approval. The first award was to the Boston Museum, followed by others that successfully generated publicity and increased private funding for all of the arts programs.

Another request for my input was an invitation to speak in closed sessions with the Endowment's new recruits to staff start-up projects. Nancy Hanks was evidently impressed with my success in bringing together "town and gown" in the Lansing/East Lansing community. A warm, kindred spirit prevailed among the participants in those sessions. I was delighted to be a player among them.

My fellow council members were mostly celebrities. At first I was quite star-struck. A perfect example of this was a knee-buckling phone call to my room following a daylong session. Jerome Robbins! The legendary choreographer and theater director had rescued my reading glasses from the cleaning crew, who were sweeping up papers left on our meeting sessions' worktables. Jerry Robbins offered to hold my specs until the council met again the next morning. I confess to being a little tongue-tied when he graciously presented them to me. I must admit that from then on, those glasses took on totemic powers.

I soon overcame my modesty and began to feel at home with these celebrated artists. Judith Jamison—dancer, choreographer, and artistic director of the Alvin Ailey Dance Company—and I would huddle over deviled eggs and salad lunches on paper plates, our paper cups

National Endowment for the Arts council member and novelist Eudora Welty and I are welcomed at dinner in the official residence of Vice President and Mrs. Walter Mondale.

half-filled with Gallo wine. A favorite conversation was venting our annoyance over the disparity between the pampered care and feeding of college football players versus the stingy attention given far-more-arduously trained dancers—ballet and modern.

And then there was Eudora Welty, author of short stories and novels, winner of the Pulitzer Prize and Presidential Medal of Freedom, with whom I sat side-by-side in many a meeting during our overlapping tenure. I recall one afternoon when Eudora adamantly addressed a controversial issue before the council in her deliberative Southern drawl. In a confidential aside, she exclaimed, "I don't know what I'm doing here."

Astonished by her self-deprecation, I protested, "Eudora, whatever you have to offer is pure, unadulterated gold to this body."

Robert Wise, Oscar-winning director of *West Side Story* and *The Sound of Music,* always silenced the room when holding forth philosophically about his filmmaking endeavors. And producer/director Harold Prince was another giant in addressing issues related to his work; for me, he personified The Theater.

Billy Taylor was an adored council member whose contributions were always beautifully articulated and wonderfully on-point, especially during controversial discussions. He was an all-time great jazz musician and historian seen regularly on *CBS Sunday Morning.* Nancy Hanks frequently called Billy into service far beyond his six-year term to use his talents when needed to counter critical arguments with unsympathetic audiences. Among the many other luminaries with whom I had memorable interactions were painter Jacob Lawrence, actress Rosalind Russell, pianist Van Cliburn, designer Charles Eames, opera diva Beverly Sills, and actor Theodore Bikel.

Equally remarkable for me was the brilliant and committed staff that made the National Endowment for the Arts function smoothly. They were the heroes and heroines who provided the intelligence and the engines for funding the creative arts in American life. Foremost was Brian O'Doherty, director of the Visual Arts and Media Arts programs and Art in Public Places. Brian, now retired, is an art historian and critic who is recognized as having had an enormously influential impact on Nancy Hanks's search for and development of aesthetic values throughout the United States.

My term on the NEA council gave me an exposure to government bureaucracy that every thinking American should experience. Ours was a cause worth fighting for. The value of the National Endowment for the Arts to the country's cultural life lies in how it enriches the wider society, providing the public with a better understanding of the strength, variety, depth and extensive richness of our American arts and culture. I was overjoyed to have had the opportunity to serve.

MY BOOK SIGNING

My friends on the faculty of the MSU Art Department had invited me to hold my initial book-signing event for *Contemporary Artists of Malaysia: A Biographic Survey* in the Kresge Art Center's main gallery on June 12, 1972. I was thrilled not only that my book had at last come to reality but also that these MSU academics were welcoming into their most exclusive club. My work was the first book about Malaysian artists, and the MSU faculty applauded me for it. My initial courtesy call at the department had grown into a mutual love affair, and I was touched by their honoring me.

Due to his heavy university schedule, Clif found it necessary to reduce his outside commitments. The MoMA board seat was one among several non-essentials from which he chose to resign. Clif had been called not as an art connoisseur but by the museum's president John Hightower, a good friend and admirer who sought Clif's administrative advice especially when MoMA was undergoing tough labor negotiations. Three years after Clif's departure, my name emerged as a candidate for board service. Given my five-year membership on MoMA's Junior Council, as well as being recognized as an ardent arts advocate, with a presidential appointment by Gerald Ford to the NEA and as a published author with my book on Malaysian art, I had visibility independent of Clif's. Nevertheless, upon receiving the letter of invitation from William Paley, chairman of MoMA's board (and founder of CBS), to become a MoMA trustee, I felt as if I had been awarded a knighthood.

Were these coveted invitations offered because I am Black or married to the MSU president? While both are obvious possibilities, I do believe that my most important accomplishment—one that continued to open doors into several renowned cultural organizations—was my deep-seated aspiration to perform with my highest potential as a caring Black woman who had witnessed a multitude of arts activities, and to work fervently with people of like interest. Arts involvement was as natural to me as if I were a tree leaning into the wind. It was not necessary to enlist my interest from outside provocateurs; rather I stepped

I chat with art faculty members Toni DeBlasi and Irv Taran at the book-signing reception for the publication of my book, *Contemporary Artists in Malaysia*. (June 12, 1972)

Signing one of my books (June 12, 1972)

repeatedly into my surroundings, wherever that happened to be, to identify the rare gems from the multitude of jewels that inspired me. I thrived on the swiftness of it all, and did so joyfully: Choosing from among those breakthrough images gave me a surge as consuming as falling in love.

Over the years I've been told by revered sages in the field, "Dolores, you have a good eye." Such accolades were flattering but for me unnecessary, as the arts are without peer in rewarding its sensitivities.

'TONIGHT'S THE NIGHT?'

As Richard Nixon's war persisted, Clif became quite proficient at using the bullhorn in responding to student demonstrators. Over the course of three years, battles raged on our campus. May and June 1970 were particularly tumultuous, with the Kent State student deaths followed by the bombing of Haiphong Harbor. Angered by reports about the killings of American and Vietnamese soldiers, and often spurred on by protest organizers, our students marched, shouted, made threats, broke windows, blocked traffic, invoked the wrath of shopkeepers, and roamed the streets of East Lansing while chanting anti-war slogans.

Their aim was to create an uprising loud enough to shut down the university in protest and force the government to end the war. Our six-year sojourn in Southeast Asia made clear to Clif and me that the U.S. intervention in the Vietnamese civil war was a flawed attempt to stop the spread of communism in the region. However, Clif was steadfast in his belief that allowing the students to close the university was an unacceptable strategy not fitting the crisis.

Clif remained determined. He never allowed the doors of the university to be closed. Given MSU's stalwart Public Safety team, he was confident that disturbances could be responsibly contained in-house. On standby was support from Governor Bill Milliken, who kept the National Guard available, proof that Clif had powerful friends ready to provide reinforcements if called. Though there was considerable structural damage on campus, Clif's foresight and wise deliberations prevailed, avoiding the excessive radicalism or loss of life suffered on other U.S. campuses.

There were attempts to take over the Administration building, the International Center, and Demonstration Hall, where many of the windows were blown out. One picture window in Cowles House had to be replaced with bulletproof glass after being shot through at a time when we were at home. During follow-up conversations with student protesters, we learned that there had been discussions targeting Cowles House for takeover. But some had asked, "What are we going to do about Mrs. Wharton? She might refuse to leave." As a result, that idea was promptly dismissed.

The chimes of the front entrance to Cowles House pulsated with repeated ringing on the night of May 18th in the minutes before 11 o'clock. They signaled a small band of raging students seeking to importune Clif to keep the Student Union open beyond its customary 11 p.m. closing.

I was alone in the residence, as Clif had joined the security forces in the campus police headquarters who were tracking hordes of students trashing and breaking the windows of university buildings in their attempt to shut down the school in protest against the war in Vietnam. Similar actions were unfolding at colleges and universities across the nation. Following their assaults on our campus, the militant students would volley back and forth between their nightly raids and the Student Union, which they considered their inviolable safe space.

Upon my arrival at the door, the students cried out, "We are discussing racism–a cause you and President Wharton should want us to continue." One blond co-ed insisted, "As Black people you and Dr. Wharton must realize the importance of our talks and allow us to stay in the Student Union." I responded with amused mockery, reaching for a head scarf from the pocket of my gingham skirt, which I donned Aunt Jemima-style. In an exaggerated Southern accent, I said, "Lorsie me! Us Black folks bin fightin' racism for over 300 years and tonight you childrens wanna talk 'bout racism, so that means TONIGHT'S THE NIGHT for racial change?" Resuming my normal voice, I added, "Sorry, my dear young people, but keeping the Union open for you tonight is just not going to happen!"

The lass pulled at her hair in frustration over the failure of her foolish pretense and retreated to the Student Union. I shook my head in disbelief and slipped back into Cowles House, my thoughts turning to my husband and the challenges of *his* evening.

By the next morning, one hundred and thirty-two students and non-students in the Student Union had been arrested for the property damage. Though we sympathized with the students in their struggle against the war, closing the university was antithetical to our resolve, and in the end Clif's order to keep the University open prevailed. For both of us, it had been one more event-filled day that defined our lives at MSU.

MARCH BY CANDLE LIGHT

If some days were unsettling, so many other were exhilarating. Partly fulfilling my role in loco parentis, I joined a group of students who had organized a candlelight march in the name of peace and caring. They wished to demonstrate their desire to engage the greater East Lansing community in bearing witness to their hatred of the war. It was to be a true town-and-gown parade that would circle the main streets of East Lansing and then proceed to the campus. Clif had been asked to lead the procession, but when the day arrived, my dear husband was flat-out exhausted from the unrelentingly strenuous events. Thus I stood alone to greet the students on the steps of Cowles House, explaining, "President Wharton has spent several days and even an overnight in the police headquarters dealing with the continuing demonstrations. He is completely burnt out and is finally resting. So I ask, will you accept me in his place tonight?"

The crowd cheered its approval, and two more candles were lit—one for me and one for Clifton 3rd. Our son, home for his second weekend

Clif and I speak to MSU student demonstrators. (May 1972)

from Dalton, stood calmly on the sidelines, wondering what was going down this time. Still the observer, Clifton joined in the spirit of the song "Give Peace a Chance" as he walked agreeably beside me and the several hundred others. We passed the music building, a gymnasium, the Administration Building, and lastly arrived at the auditorium, where the protest was to conclude.

By coincidence, more than a thousand students were just leaving the auditorium following a rock concert. The two groups could not have been more opposite, one carrying candles in soulful observance of peace on earth, the other bleary-eyed from high-strung music and God-knows-what-else. Town and gown had come together, all right, in the name of embracing the spirit of "Give Peace a Chance." The moment characterized my life as a participant in a deeply engaged population on an American university campus in the 1970s.

Our campus police, many of them students themselves in Public Safety studies, were known to go the extra mile to avoid arresting their on-campus brothers and sisters, whereas the Lansing and East Lansing authorities were annoyed with the students' misdeeds, regardless of their well-meaning anti-war intentions.

One sunny spring afternoon, a huge contingent of students, perhaps a couple of thousand or more, began a nonviolent march to the State Capitol to present their demands against the war. Much to their chagrin, the student leaders had failed to obtain a permit to walk through the streets from East Lansing to the Capitol. Lt. Heywood Julian of the MSU police, concerned that the Lansing police might arrest the students, strode boldly in front of the marchers leading the demonstration. Julian, a tall and imposing man in uniform who was the very model of a law enforcer, disabused his police comrades of any notion of confronting one of their own. Thus, the students marched and finally arrived in front of the Michigan Legislature building, where they vented their anger and stated their demands. With mission accomplished, they dispersed and Julian returned to campus police barracks, a slight grin of satisfaction replacing his customary stern expression.

I confront a demonstration leader of the protest. (May 1972)

I often met on the steps of Cowles House with angry students, individually and in groups as large as a hundred or more. They wanted the president and me to understand their outrage over the reports of napalm bombs, people brutalized, and children maimed and orphaned in Vietnam. On a number of occasions, I invited the protesters into our residence, where we talked for hours.

During those conversations, my own anguish flared as I recalled the many joy-filled events during my several riveting visits—pre-war—to Vietnam. I loved waking at dawn under a mosquito net blowing in the soft air in a simple wood-frame hotel in the ancient capital of Hue. From an unpainted hotel window I had watched hundreds of beautiful girls and women riding bicycles to work, dressed in traditional white pajamas covered by ankle-length panels of bright pastel silks, their high-neck Mandarin collars framing doll-like faces shaded beneath cone-shaped straw hats. The scene deserved poetry as touching as Emily Dickinson's "The Butterfly upon the Sky."

I made three trips to Vietnam with Clif, who was administering ADC grants to university educators there. Now seated in our Cowles House living room, speaking with students about the war, my memory flashed back to Trai Le, dean of the University of Hue law school, and her husband, the Provost, both providing strong leadership to their university. The erudite couple were physically small and gentle but intellectually huge in discussing the economy of their country and efforts to expand the scholarship of the young minds so eager to receive an advanced education.

The grace of Vietnamese culture was highlighted one evening when Trai and Chan Le honored us with a typical Vietnamese river cruise dinner outing. Clif and I floated along in an open *sampan* on the Perfume River, as I let my fingers glide in calm waters as servants fastidiously prepared a seven-course dinner in another *sampan* rocking gently beside us. Melodious string music from a third *sampan* charmed the night. All this loveliness captivated our hearts, while our hosts, in a fourth *sampan,* delighted over our obvious appreciation of the way of life in their country.

On another afternoon, I recalled being escorted by a faculty member to several abandoned ancient palaces. We strolled past magnificently sculpted stone lions, huge three-legged bronze urns decorated with legendary stories from ages long past, multitiered temple rooftops, small pagodas set upon man-made lakes where the male royalty would withdraw for hours on end to write poetry. Leading me farther along a dusty road, my guide brought me to a simple wooden cabin from which emanated muffled drumming. Inside was a group of about fourteen young girls dancing. They were students rehearsing the famed choreography recounting a true story of Vietnamese heroines who had fought victoriously against Chinese invaders. This period of Vietnamese history was unknown to most U.S. military policy makers.

Heartsick as I sat in Cowles House reliving my experiences in Vietnam, I thought to myself, "Oh, that those graceful and courageous heroines could have endured to this day, fighting Vietnam's enemies so gallantly." All of this was a stunning contrast to newsreels showing the people of Vietnam screaming as they ran from our American warriors and the hell they came to symbolize. How could this be? The thought of these young American students seated on our soft carpet being sent by our government to carry guns and bayonets to the peaceful villages of Vietnam was unbearable to me.

A very different flashback reminded me of a dinner party in our Singapore home when the somewhat-intoxicated wife of a British diplomat blasted my ear with, "Vietnam is going to blow to kingdom come, and you Americans don't have a clue about what you are actually doing to that country!"

Truly, the U.S. officials did prove themselves amateurs in Asian diplomacy in comparison to the British and the French. The impression wasn't helped when the CIA, attempting to eavesdrop on intelligence between the British and the new Singapore government, overloaded the electrical circuits in Singapore's Goodwood Park Hotel one night in 1960 and created a major blackout that affected the entire island. The American consul general became the laughingstock of the island in the wake of weeklong repairs to the downtown Singapore electrical system.

These and other experiences were background to my discussions with distraught students that went on for many a night. Our conversations served to quell some of the anger demonstrated by my visitors and accordingly their call for Clif to close the university.

It was a mystery to many journalists that very few of MSU's Black students were seen marching against the war. Their response to being wooed into the protest marches was, "We have no fight against the Vietnamese!" The MSU student Strike Committee added several possible issues in an attempt to attract the Black students. One was the case of Bobby Seale, a Black Panther leader who had been imprisoned for his

Professors James and
Ruth Hamilton "The Finest
of the Fine!"

role in the Chicago Democratic National Convention riots. Another was
the demand that 16 percent of the student body be composed of Blacks
by autumn 1971. But with an ongoing independent voice, the Black students remained aloof.

A group of Black collegiate activists, eager to decorate a Black student
center, approached me to assist in obtaining art for a room in one of
the dorms that Clif had designated for them. "Mrs. Wharton, we would
like to hang some Afro-American art on the walls of our Black Students
Cultural Room."

Delighted, I asked, "What do you have in mind? We might be able to
find photographs or posters. How about prints by leading Black painters
such as Romare Bearden or Jacob Lawrence? I'll be pleased to check
out the Studio Art Museum in Harlem and the Barnes Collection in
Philadelphia to see what art they have in their shops."

The students replied with enthusiasm that either artist would be perfect for their conference center.

After a search that was great good fun for me, I produced twenty
Bearden lithographs of Black children at play in city life, which were
mounted on poster boards for hanging. As I helped the students develop
the space, our friendships flourished, beginning a long-running conversation about themselves and their other involvements on campus.

The richness of the Black presence within MSU was strong. Soon after arriving at the university, I became deeply interested in the research of Professor Ruth Hamilton, a Black sociology scholar who pioneered the study of the African Diaspora—the movement and migration of African people around the globe. Ruth's sudden death in 2003 was to me the loss of an important human being who stood tall among countless individuals I most admired, respected, and loved during my lifetime. She and her husband, Jim, a professor of chemistry and assistant provost, were paragons of academic and pedagogical excellence. To this day, thousands in the university community lament their absence.

I listen to residents in McDonel Hall during one of several weeklong overnight visits to women's dormitories. (April 19, 1971)

Clifton and I preside at MSU's 11th Annual Staff Retirement and Service Recognition Dinner on March 23, 1973. Our joy at working together is readily apparent—even at official functions.

Launching my annual program of recognizing widows of MSU faculty and staff (June 19, 1973)

Trustee Lloyd Cofer reads the citation as Central Michigan University bestows on me an Honorary Doctorate of Humane Letters—my first of nine honorary degrees. (May 12, 1973)

Sorority members congratulate me following my induction as Honorary Soror of the AKA Sorority, the nation's first formally organized Black Greek sisterhood. (April 22, 1977)

Betty Ford and I take off for the MSU Museum, after overnight visit at Cowles House. (Sept. 16, 1976)

"Three First Ladies" visit the MSU Museum. Left to right: me, U.S. First Lady Betty Ford; Museum Director Kent Dewhurst; Museum Curator Marsha McDowell; Michigan First Lady Helen Milliken. (Sept. 16, 1976)

THE LISTENING POSTS

Soon after the demonstrations ended, Larry Boger, dean of agriculture and a strong member of Clif's brain trust, pressed Clif to reach out to the curious, the doubters, and the fence-sitters over his leadership of their revered MSU. Larry's strength of personality, imposing baritone voice, and farm background gave him valuable entrée among the state's powerful agricultural families, which included many MSU alumni, as well as business and community leaders. Speaking as a wise counselor, Larry knew that Clif would win the respect of the citizenry were they given the opportunity to see and hear him in action. A two-year schedule of "Listening Posts" visits was arranged—not unlike those prepared for statewide political campaigns. Accompanied by a small entourage of university administrators and their spouses, we met with some twenty different audiences around Michigan. Clif was the principal performer and I his adjunct as we addressed the state of the university, campus unrest caused by the raging Vietnam War, MSU's People's Park (where demonstrating students camped out for weeks), increased tuition, and drugs.

During those chaotic times, I made three visits to the women's dormitories as guest in residence, living in-house for a week each time. I became well-educated during evening rap sessions, seated on the floor among groups of young women as they shared heartfelt concerns and troubling arguments. They all were seeking creative answers to national and global issues as well as a few personal unmentionables. These experiences were meaningful to me, especially in providing real insights to share with the "Listening Posts" audiences.

We won a lot of friends, but Clif's adversaries persisted. The dissident trustees who fought his initial appointment continued their pernicious stunts to embarrass and oust him. One memorable and embittered quote made to Clif soon after our arrival at MSU was, "Wharton, don't unpack!" Whether it was leaking the salaries of university personnel or attacking Clif's efforts to enhance MSU's research capabilities, no subject was too big or small—as long as it had the potential to damage my husband's image. For his part, Clif countered every move with calm intelligence, so much so that after one contentious board meeting, the student *State News* headline trumpeted, "Wharton Wins Again."

Beyond Clif's frequent appearances on campus, he easily averaged ten speeches a month before Michigan-based and national audiences. My husband was clear in his requests to have me accompany him, my calendar permitting. I was happy to join him, part of a vital force as he fought to survive within a demanding public arena. Clif's quest was to steady a ship he'd taken over when it already was under pressure from student unrest, disputes over minority admissions, budget reductions, and more. Those problems aside, his highest aspiration was to further enhance MSU's standing among major American universities. Whatever the immediate issue, Clif's erudition was always clear and sincere in conversations that revealed the training of a scholar in command of his subject. My role as his partner evolved, expanding from my earlier, more modest efforts in Asia to a higher level of significant participation at MSU. And I loved it.

CAMPUS ENRICHMENT CAMPAIGN

Before our arrival at MSU, campaigning for private dollars had not been a high priority at the university. There were legitimate concerns that the state Legislature might use that unreliable outside revenue stream as an excuse to reduce its appropriation to the university. Clif felt strongly that MSU needed to build its private base like other public universities, but he approached new initiatives very carefully.

"Music, Lasagna with Van Cliburn" is how *Detroit Free Press* columnist Jeanne Whittaker described the world-renowned pianist's late evening with guests in our home. (April 19, 1971)

One of his first efforts was to increase the membership of the President's Club from sixty-one individuals to a number befitting its importance to this mega-university. We developed an annual program that included MSU campus–related tours for President's Club members, with each event concluding at a Cowles House reception. Our thought was to embrace the members' support and, at the same time, express our appreciation for their gifts by showcasing specifically for their benefit some of the university's most recent innovations. By 1976 the number of members stood at over four hundred.

We got the ball rolling with a capital campaign not previously attempted at MSU. The start-up for the drive began at the November 1971 Board of Trustees meeting with Clif's persuasive introduction asking for approval of a new performing arts center along with several smaller projects. The center would replace the existing auditorium, a dismal place, and accordingly advance the arts at MSU.

In the past, such suggestions had been vehemently opposed by a highly vocal group preferring an "all-events building," which was basically a multipurpose sports facility. When a Committee on Undergraduate Education had fervently requested a new auditorium back in 1967, an outraged state senator exclaimed, "A performing arts center? I don't want to see any grown men decked out in tutus prancing across any stage in my county!"

Clif's vision won the day, and the board authorized the creation of MSU's first major fund drive, the Campus Enrichment Campaign. To my great delight the performing arts center was to be the project's major component. Recalling that sea-change event, my friend the puppeteer, Phyllis Maner, an ardent supporter of the theater, said, "In the past a performing arts center wasn't a subject one would even raise in polite conversation in Lansing. You and Clif made the subject OK to discuss."

I was ready to accept with enthusiasm any role in the development of the performing arts center, despite my other commitments. My involvement proved to be one of the most meaningful of my time at MSU.

Phyllis Maner

CHAPTER 7

MSU's Performing Arts Center

The Campus Enrichment Campaign was MSU's first organized venture into the realm of private fund raising. Clif launched the initiative furthering the earlier outreach programs such as the Listening Post tours, increasing the President's Club membership, and playing nice with the local businesses, many of which were fed-up with our students trashing their property. Clif brought onto his administrative team a former MSU officer turned corporate CEO, Les Scott, as vice president for development to orchestrate the fund-raising drive. In November 1972 Bob Perrin, vice president for external affairs and one of Clif's central advisors, produced a film, "A Place to Grow," featuring Clif and me calling for support for the new center. Clif's message and clarion call: "Any great university worthy of the mantle requires a strong arts dimension—a feature that has been neglected at MSU." I, as a recognized champion of the arts in general and the new center in particular, urged support from the university's various constituents.

Clif asked the provost, John Cantlon, to organize a committee to study the successes and blunders of other universities that had recently built performing arts facilities. Cantlon appointed five MSU faculty stalwarts and me as the Architecture Visiting Committee. Then he tasked us with touring a collection of carefully selected, architecturally significant university theater facilities to determine what structural features we did and did not want.

At the committee's first meeting, I stressed the importance of investigating the designs of recent innovative architectural developments, suggesting that even London, England, be included among the locations to visit—a feeler that John Cantlon promptly countered with, "Dolores, I'm prepared to give you a long leash, but not that long."

Thus, in 1972 our eager fact-finding team, traveling together and sometimes separately, surveyed sixteen centers and thirty theaters around the U.S. The visits included University of Illinois's Krannert Center, Indiana University's Auditorium, Iowa State University's Stephens Auditorium, University of Akron's E.J. Thomas Hall, University of Iowa's Hancher Auditorium, and Lincoln Center's Alice Tully Hall.

A key member of our committee was Ken Beachler, director of the Lecture Concert Series at the old auditorium, who opened the doors to his "club" of fellow theater impresarios. Through them we learned what worked, what were the pitfalls, what inspired, what mistakes and calamities to avoid. For example, one director told of a design oversight in which a completed million-dollar parking lot led patrons to the theater's backstage rather than its main entrance. Another surprise lay waiting when, soon before opening night, it was discovered that the architects had forgotten to include a box office for selling tickets. Every university host who received us spoke of inadequate space given to ladies' rooms.

Acoustic quality was the most critical and unpredictable building issue. At that time, music halls with seating capacity under 1,800 could be scientifically controlled, but those with larger numbers were trickier. With the seating capacity for our planned MSU center estimated at 2,500, acoustics was of primary interest during our investigations. I was so indoctrinated over the issue that even years afterward, when entering an empty theater, I've felt the urge to clap my hands robustly to test the sound feedback. Lighting and thousands of other high-tech issues onstage, backstage, inside, and outside each facility were thoroughly examined. Our note-taking was voluminous.

Following each visit, we would compare notes and reactions to the various projects over dinner. We also would share our individual aspirations for the center. My wish was that the facility be an ideal instrument allowing emotions to soar under the spell of great performances. Ken Beachler wanted its two theaters to function perfectly, seducing his audiences to return again and again. Jim Niblock, true to his role as chair of the music department, asked for a sound so pure every note could be heard distinctly in each seat of the two auditoriums.

Anne Garrison, professor of business law, wanted a theater in which she might exchange her dress shoes for bedroom slippers, relax in comfortable seats, and disappear into a world rich in classical music and drama. Frank Rutledge, chair of the Theater Department, thought the status quo was just fine! His reaction surprised none of us, as he was always the committee contrarian and at the center of virtually every disagreement. But every one of us held the deepest wishes for the shining ideal for Michigan State's audiences. And we also knew that the university and broader community would support our lofty goals.

How did we know? Because history was on our side: Whatever its shortcomings, the old auditorium hosted countless unforgettable performances by world-famous artists on tour, often with a luncheon, reception, or dinner party in their honor at our residence.

Among the luminaries were ballet dancer Rudolf Nureyev, whose collaboration with Martha Graham gave us an exclusive conversation fixed in our love for modern dance; opera diva Joan Sutherland and her husband/accompanist, the renowned conductor Richard Bonynge (their dinner party gave me a near-coronary when I discovered our secretary had forgotten to include Clif and me at our own table honoring the couple, a potential catastrophe that we managed to head off just in the nick of time); pianist/conductor Daniel Barenboim and his wife, cellist Jacqueline du Pré, who together gave a legendary performance; choreographer Alvin Ailey, who recalled warmly our celebration of his company in our Kuala Lumpur home; composer and band leader Duke Ellington, who dedicated his performance of "Satin Doll" to me before a packed house; pianist Vladimir Horowitz; violinist Isaac Stern; and certainly neither last nor least, Fort Worth, Texas' own classical superstar, pianist Van Cliburn, who became a dear friend during our tenure as council members on the National Endowment for the Arts and who graciously agreed to be MSU's fall 1974 commencement speaker.

Clif and I would invite a who's who of the greater Lansing community to welcome our superstars—it was a win/win situation that made Cowles House a crossroads where town-and-gown notables could meet and interact. Not only did this social interaction with visiting celebrities enhance the university's image of distinction and broaden its reputation, it built a greater appreciation for the arts across Michigan and helped set the stage for our new performance center. And what a time I had!

Confident that all aspects of our committee's mission had been faithfully addressed, we presented our report to John Cantlon. Construction would later begin, with Claudill Rowlett Scott architects of Houston and engineers from Harley Ellington Pierce Yee of Southfield, both contributing to the design of Wharton Center. Construction led by Christman Company of Lansing, Michigan, followed.

The performing arts center component of the fund-raising campaign needed a major public launch. But what should it be and who would organize it? Les Scott suggested a black-tie gala with a performance by a featured celebrity. Ken Beachler came back with the bright suggestion that we explore booking Tony Bennett and Lena Horne, as the famed duo had recently concluded an acclaimed run on Broadway with their show "Tony & Lena Sing."

At this point I thought that Faculty Folk would be the perfect co-sponsors for the event. For several years, I had had the pleasure of organizing campus tours for the Faculty Folk membership, using some of the rights and privileges of my First Ladyship to open doors to behind-the-scenes activities and facilities not normally accessible to others.

These included the complexity of the dormitory kitchens, showing how some eighteen thousand students were fed a nourishing, safe, and efficiently prepared daily diet while living in the dorms; the operation of our gargantuan power plant facilities; a drive through the research farms on the southern part of the eight-square-mile campus, observing such experimental projects as the cross-breeding of ferocious mink with milder-mannered ferrets to create a more gentle breed of pups; and even tours of the four-lake complex where wastewater was purified.

Once it was agreed upon to approach the Faculty Folk as possible co-sponsors, I revamped my yearly campus tour for the group with an added twist: a walkabout to show the inadequacy of the old auditorium that used a single stage to serve two theaters—a 3,700-seat general assembly hall on one side of the stage, with the 600-seat Fairchild Theatre on the other. For that particular facility tour, I copied the practice of the London theater vendors who walked the aisles during intermission selling chips and sandwiches. For my event, I replaced the tawdry British hawkers with dolled-up student waitresses offering delicately packaged chocolates on fancy trays that were suspended from their necks with wide velvet ribbons. This little piece of theatrics-for-a-good-cause well serve to inspire the ladies' interest in a new performing arts center.

A few days after the auditorium walkabout, I extended my annual invitation to the Faculty Folk Executive Committee to discuss their next outing as my guests. But this time, I laid the seeds for a new game plan, saying, "As a start-up for the Campus Enrichment Campaign to raise private funds for a new performing arts center, plans are under way for a fund-raising event." I paused for effect, finally continuing, "Under consideration is a gala black-tie evening featuring the famed Broadway duo, 'Tony and Lena Sing'! Such a dramatic and glamourous event should attract a wide audience." Then, looking directly at each of my sedately attentive guests, I asked, "Would Faculty Folk be willing to take on the event as its organizer and presenter?"

Silence stilled the air for every bit of twenty seconds before even a sigh of surprise or a clearing of the throat was made. Finally, the organization's president, Lil Smuckler, turned away from my questioning smile and sought a reaction from her three colleagues, who in unison, as if wired together, looked back to Lil. Another few seconds passed before Lil finally regained her breath and replied, "This would be a major undertaking. We have never before considered such a responsibility or challenge. We will have to take this up with the membership before responding."

The others, expressionless, nodded very slowly in agreement. Before bidding me goodbye, each committee member said privately, "We'll get back to you soon, Dolores."

Had my life depended on voicing an opinion regarding the Faculty Folk's decision, I could not have possibly provided it. I knew that each of these women truly loved the university. But the club's activities had historically centered on promoting fellowship among members, awarding scholarships, volunteering staff for the medical clinic, and furthering recreational, charitable, and educational objectives. Would they, could they, go so far as to take on a major fund-raising event for MSU? I didn't have a clue and was a little uneasy about where I might turn next, were they to refuse.

A few days later, I answered the phone and breathed a great sigh of relief when Lil Smuckler declared, "The membership has decided to take on the benefit." And indeed, they did! The club worked hand-in-hand

Faculty Folk president
Lil Smuckler

Faculty Folk leadership and stalwart organizers of the "Tony and Lena Sing" gala:
Lotta Hunt, Clare Byerrum, and Frankie Boger

with the fund-raising professionals, and what had once been a well-established wives general service club transformed itself into a juggernaut. The ladies organized, planned, communicated, designed, spoke publicly, hosted at-home dinner parties before concerts, and so much more. It was a game changer that hit like a whirlwind, resulting in a benefit with $100 tickets—three times the prices of the past. "Outrageous!" cried some. "Brava!" shouted others.

CALM AFTER THE STORM

Event night, April 19, 1975, brought a traumatic real-life storm that threatened the success of the evening. It began several days before the benefit with a steady rainfall that became torrential just hours before the curtain was to rise. As the storm kicked up in volume and velocity, it caused the Red Cedar River to overflow, flooding many areas, including the Auditorium and its power grid. Lena Horne was on the stage rehearsing when we received the official word: "It is impossible for the building to be used this evening!"

Lena Horne and Tony Bennett join us at the MSU Faculty Club as we celebrate their brilliant fund-raising concert. (April 19, 1975)

After months of planning, huge monetary investments, and musicians poised to play, we found ourselves in a hair-pulling panic. What to do? On-site, two of Clif's officers suggested they switch the venue to the recently constructed ice hockey arena. Without hesitation, Clif replied, "Let's go for it!"

The people of Michigan State University have an uncanny drive for reaching beyond the credible to achieve their goal. Countless segments of the university and their relentless crews went into high gear to change the location for the concert: A carpeted stage was built on top of the ice; theatrical lighting was installed; seating was remapped from one facility to the other; ushers were trained in the new floor plan and seating as-signments; transportation was arranged between the flooded auditori-um and the hockey arena for those ticket holders unaware of the move; detail after detail was thought through to meet every possible need and eventuality. And what seemed a Sisyphean task was successfully completed in a few very-short hours. Lena Horne's and Tony Bennett's dazzling concert was actually heightened in exhilaration as they, too, re-sponded to the celebration of a catastrophe deftly avoided. Miraculously and beautifully, the gala was a brilliant success.

Clif and I were grateful for the protective care of the Almighty when falling into bed that night. But the real heroes of the benefit were the la-dies of Faculty Folk who had accepted the initial charge; MSU faculty and administrators who were undaunted by the challenge; and the teams of people who faced unexpected catastrophes against an impossible physical adversity. We praised many compatriots from all over Mid-Michigan for their clear response to the call for a new performing arts center.

NEW HORIZONS

By 1977 there were mounting rumors that Clif was being wooed by other universities. Now recognized widely as having a strong presence within the ranks of university presidents, he had proven his leadership acumen. A summary of his achievements included the design of a new MSU governance structure, coping with the intricacies of an NCAA football investigation, and meeting the most recent demand imposed upon

Mel Leiserowitz of the MSU art department stands in front of his sculpture "Orpheus," installed on the Wharton Center grounds. (April 19, 1975)

Clif announces his resignation at a farewell press conference in the MSU board room. (Oct. 27, 1977)

university presidents—raising money—for which he launched MSU's first fund-raising drive. But perhaps the most telling demonstrations of his intellect were made obvious in his speeches at national academic meetings and conferences. Therein he set forth his views on the issues facing higher education.

So it was hardly surprising that Clif's name began to appear on lists of candidates under consideration to head other universities. Clif ignored most of these approaches. Nevertheless, though the three notoriously dissident trustees eventually left the board, a few others frustrated Clif's hands-on efforts, making more secure career prospects increasingly attractive. The sixty-four-campus State University of New York, built up by Governor Nelson Rockefeller, appeared worth exploring, especially given Clif's positive experience working for the Rockefellers in his early career. Not long after the SUNY board search committee visited us on campus, Clif's name appeared at the top of SUNY's short list of possible leaders. The decision-making process by the giant institution was swift in offering Clif the SUNY chancellorship. Clif's response in accepting was equally rapid.

The one and only time I attended a Michigan State University Board of Trustees meeting was on October 26, 1977, when Clif announced he was leaving MSU to become chancellor of the State University of New York. For me, the move to SUNY was far more than bittersweet—it was heart-wrenching. Over the years, I had come to identify personally with MSU. In fact, I remain highly sentimental about my years there. My one regret was that the timing did not allow us to complete the fund-raising drive for the performing arts center. Fortunately, the momentum was such that the campaign's Honorary Chair John Hannah and his lieutenants were able to step into the breach and bring the building to a reality.

As a postscript, more than four years later, on April 2, 1982, Clif and I were at a SUNY dinner when he was called to the phone. Gone briefly, he returned to our table and whispered in my ear, "Have I got a *big* surprise for you! It was [MSU trustee] Blanche Martin on the phone. MSU had its board meeting today. They named the performing arts center for us!"

We had not returned to Michigan since leaving in 1978, as Clif, like John Hannah before him, believed it inappropriate to interrupt the start-up of new leadership. For us, inherent in the Board of Trustees' announcement, was the knowledge that our names were to be permanently inscribed within the heart of Michigan State University with: "The Clifton and Dolores Wharton Center for the Performing Arts." I was overwhelmed.

The dedication took place September 25–26, 1982. The great hall, now the Catherine Herrick Cobb Great Hall, holds wide rows of 2,500 seats in regal gold that curve gracefully across the enormous auditorium where each side is met by handsome white columns as statuesque as Rodin sculptures. The hum and buzz resounded with excitement during the opening event. University principals, state officials, community potentates, major benefactors, our son Bruce and his date—everyone, it seemed, was on-hand for the opening of this handsome house dedicated to the performing arts. Adding to the glory of the celebration was a performance by the Chicago Symphony Orchestra with the soprano Birgit Nilsson as soloist.

Cecil Mackey, then president of MSU, extended a gracious welcome to the audience befitting this stunning occasion and offered laudatory compliments about Clif's and my part in laying the groundwork for the center. Following our introduction by Board Chairman John Bruff, I spoke first:

There is one thing that every true Spartan knows: Above everything else, Michigan State is more than a university. It is a way of life. Clif and I came to East Lansing, and through those years, we discovered a world—a world for us that was larger, it was richer, it was warmer. Michigan State will

Clif and I attend the dedication of the Clifton & Dolores Wharton Center for Performing Arts accompanied by Director Kenneth Beachler. (September 25, 1982).

MSU President Emeritus John Hannah and his wife, Sarah, embrace me with warm congratulations at the Wharton Center dedication.

always be a part of what we are. We are deeply moved by your generosity in allowing us to remain a part of you.

Then Clif stepped forward, saying:

I suppose that in everyone's life there are moments that stand out in high relief, memories that carry an extraordinary charge of emotion. In my life and that of my family, a disproportionate number of those moments happened at MSU.

What could be more thrilling than our first introduction to the vastness of the university, even before my appointment had taken effect—standing on the fifty-yard line in Spartan Stadium in front of 77,500 football fans, total strangers everyone, but all applauding with typical MSU warmth? . . .

What could have been more wrenching than leaving at last, and announcing at a press conference that decision, so enormous that up to that very moment neither Dolores nor I ourselves quite believed it was true?

Moving moments, every one of them: moments whose meaning and resonance remain fresh through all the intervening years. Yet this moment—now, today, this minute—simultaneously re-enriches and surpasses them all.

The audience's response was for me a transcendent lifetime moment, as if I were being raised and buoyed in space while a hundred violins played crescendos in the background. The Center for Performing Arts had become a reality—and with enormous acceptance by a wide community that welcomed it wholeheartedly.

Adolphus Hailstork,
composer

Mike Brand, Executive Director,
Wharton Center. *Harley Seeley,
Photographer.*

James Forger,
Dean, College of
Music

Years have passed since that incredible, joyful night. I now look back recalling an intriguing history. James Forger, Dean of the College of Music,
and Michael Brand, Executive Director of the Wharton Center commissioned Adolphus Hailstork, a highly regarded composer and MSU graduate, to honor Clifton and me with a new work as part of the dedication.
Drawing on romantic poems by Percy Bysshe Shelly, Hailstork titled his
full length orchestral production, "Serenade: To Hearts Which Near Each
Other Move"—a sentiment that could not have been more appropriate,
both to Clif and me, and to the occasion.

The heights to which the Center has grown are the result of a series of individual maestros who have guided the Center's development.
During the early 2000s the inspired commitment and support by MSU
President Lou Anna Simon was steadfast allowing Michael Brand break-
away outreach. Beginning in 2004, Brand has held the mantle as director

November 2, 2015 offered another choice occasion in my memorabilia at MSU. President Lou Anna Simon interviewed me on stage at the Wharton Center. Central to our conversation, she asked, "Dolores, if you were to say in a few words why Michigan State was special to you . . . what would it be?" I, without hesitation, replied, "The ready acceptance to creativity and excellence . . . while recognizing what I wanted to achieve."

of Wharton Center, a position he commands to this day. The breadth of his influence has permeated other Michigan cultural institutions, drawing them into the Center's purview. I am soaring with pride in what has come to pass at the Wharton Center for the Performing Arts and the extraordinary people who have elevated it.

Wharton Center facade with focus on a 39' x 27' hanging banner characterizing the ART found at WhARTon Center in 2017.

CHAPTER 8

State University of New York

Prominent on the commercial bus tours circling downtown Albany was a stop at SUNY headquarters. Formerly the home of the Delaware and Hudson Railroad, it is a gray-stone homage to the Cloth Hall in Ypres, Belgium, with gothic gargoyles, parapets, and majestic two-story windows. The tour guides would announce that Clifton Wharton, the new chancellor of the State University of New York, and his wife, Dolores, chose to make their home in the South Tower of this recently restored office building. Furthermore, tourists would wonder at the site, perhaps asking themselves, "Why would they want to move into an area centered in Albany's red-light district and a Jesus Saves mission?"

For me, the South Tower was a designer's paradise, with marvelous views of the Hudson River to the east and Albany's Empire State Plaza with its stunning egg-shaped theater to the west. The complex of state office buildings was an exquisite symbol of New York State's grandeur as conceived by then-Governor Nelson Rockefeller and Wallace Harrison, architect of the United Nations Secretariat building and the Metropolitan Opera House at Lincoln Center.

The seventh floor of our triplex apartment was designated for entertaining, with its reconstruction engineered by Elwin Stevens, the university architect, and with me selecting contemporary furnishings that dramatically complemented the exterior facade of imposing Gothic stonework. So as not to impose on the taxpayers, we funded the furnishing of the South Tower residence through a donation of Clif's corporate fees to the university. The deftly drawn, angular rooms were decorated in white and beige, with wood panels of light-grained oak, ceiling-to-floor raw-silk draperies puddling onto plush carpeting, marble and glass tabletops accented with my great-grandfather's heirlooms of silver and cut glass, and a family treasure—a French porcelain punch bowl—dominating the dining room. I brought large paintings from our personal collection, including *Judy's Boy* (acrylic on canvas) by MSU's Irv Taran, *Chairman Mao* (lithograph) by Andy Warhol, and a Pablo Picasso lithograph.

Our South Tower became a showplace for receiving Albany politicians, with Governor Hugh Carey asking us to invite his guests, confirming that a contemporary presence could be found in stodgy old Albany. Countless out-of-town business leaders, local cultural groups, and many of our university family from the sixty-four campuses were welcomed by the chancellor to SUNY headquarters at our apartment. The residence was doubly applauded, as the area had in recent years been abandoned by the city's former established society. Our arrival signaled the beginning of gentrification. If our South Tower lights were shining at night, friends honked three short toots of their car horns as they drove on the arterial overpasses that circled the south end of our building. It was an exhilarating place, alluring and sophisticated. Acceptance of the new family at home in our daring new residence was joy-filled. But it had not started out that way.

Our new setting was a striking contrast to the lifestyle we experienced at Michigan State University:

MSU: A single campus of five-thousand-plus acres.

SUNY: A network of sixty-four individual campuses spread across the state.

MSU: A 160-year-old institution respected for its dedication to agriculture and the enrichment of the lives of people throughout the Midwest and beyond.

SUNY: A recent groundbreaking venture uniting a heterogeneous group of research universities, four-year colleges, community colleges, and medical schools into a single system funded by the taxpayers of the state of New York.

MSU Board: Often difficult, with several members openly obstreperous in their dealings with Clif.

SUNY Board: Embraced my husband from the start as their own leader-extraordinaire of higher education.

Panoramic view of SUNY Plaza, with our South Tower home on the right.

MSU: Honored its First Lady with deference and ever-ready applause as she stood beside the president.

SUNY: "Lady, will you please find yourself someplace else to go!"—the welcome implied by old-line insiders such as SUNY's secretary to the board, who received me like a bag of wet diapers.

Be assured, I had arrived at SUNY with an already-full professional agenda. I was committed to routine travel for my corporate boards—Phillips Petroleum in Bartlesville, Oklahoma; Kellogg Company in Battle Creek, Michigan; New York Telephone Company, later renamed NYNEX, in Manhattan (following the generous transfer of my board membership by Michigan Bell)—council meetings of the National Endowment for the Arts in Washington, DC, and trustee meetings at MoMA in the center of the cultural universe, New York City.

Then there were the immediate domestic demands of packing and unpacking, complicated by a temporary move into the former chancellor's home on Marion Avenue. Before Clif had accepted the chancellorship, the SUNY board had promised us a new residence. Alas, the search required weeks of house hunting throughout the Albany environs, during which we saw nothing suitable. To our great delight, during an unrelated visit to the new SUNY headquarters, still under construction, we visited the smaller of two towers on the south end of the building, which had been designated for office space. The tower's physical features were easily accommodating to alteration. Could it be renovated as a residence, we wondered? Oscar Lanford, vice chancellor for capital facilities, was intrigued with the idea and said, "Let's explore it." And so we did, ultimately deciding that, rather than purchase new real estate, we would renovate the tower as our home and a showcase to entertain SUNY's many and varied guests.

In the interim, we were obliged to live in the Marion Avenue residence, a house owned by the university and previously imposed upon the former chancellor, Ernie Boyer, who claimed that the best part of retiring was leaving that house. The interior was dark, creepy, and overbearing, with low ceilings and many windowless rooms—a perfect setting for a Stephen King novel or *Addams Family* TV show. Instead of the man-servant Lurch clumsily meandering about, it was I who was left to rustle up a cozy homestead out of the scary Marion Avenue Mansion, as it was often called. On my first day alone I explored the premises, stopping in the kitchen where, set in the middle of a Formica table, stood a not-too-clean sugar bowl. Curious, I lifted the lid to discover a crispy, long-legged, long-deceased cockroach. I was overcome with revulsion. Was this little horror intended as a welcoming joke for the new chancellor and his wife?

I put my head in my hands and let out a long, loud groan.

Though I attempted to take the Marion Avenue layover in stride, I did feel unfairly wounded by an article in the *Times Union*, the main newspaper for the Albany area. The headline read: "Chancellor's wife refuses mansion set within Albany's finest residential neighborhood." To me, the write-up described an arrogant and difficult woman for whom the SUNY authorities would be forced to buy new property. Though such criticism is not unexpected for life in the public eye, this introduction into the Albany community required some tough minded determination.

Such an image was a reversal of my role in Clif's and my wonderfully compatible and adventurous marriage. Previously, I had welcomed each of our life-changing transitions: working, exploring, parenting, enjoying our sons and ourselves. This new round, however, was off to a rocky start!

Another discomforting encounter within the SUNY family took place at a small dinner party given by Board Chairman Elisabeth Luce Moore and her husband, Maurice "Tex" Moore. They were both super-establishment, super-wealthy, and ruling aristocrats. Beth's brother, Henry Luce, was the founder of Time Inc., and Tex was founding partner of New York City's hotshot law firm Cravath, Swaine & Moore. Our hosts brought us together for an intimate evening with Nelson and Happy Rockefeller. Nelson was the former governor of New York, who had also served as vice president under Gerald Ford and was appropriately recognized as the father of SUNY. Furthermore, Clif's association with Nelson was long standing. For starters, Clif had been one among a select few of Nelson's bright young talents. In fact, Clif's first professional job was at the American International Association for Economic and Social Development, a not-for-profit organization of Nelson Rockefeller's, dealing in Latin America. Years later, Clif served as a member of Nelson's Presidential Mission to Latin America.

Protocol for the evening was conventionally formal, with conversation that was worldly and current. In that the table-talk frequently focused on business matters with which I was familiar, I was not shy about sharing my own insights. Then during dessert, Tex Moore turned to me and bluntly declared, "You certainly have a lot to say!" I was stunned but pretended not to hear the insult. Next, during the cheese and salad course, Tex again spoke up, telling me, "You have no business serving on those corporate boards. You should be at home caring for your husband!" I was speechless, and for the remainder of the evening I maintained a pleasant but wooden smile until the Rockefellers bade their farewells and we, too, departed.

Tex Moore's lecture left me smoldering with a third-degree burn. Obviously, I was the victim of a double standard. After all, Beth Moore was also a woman and wife and now chairman of the SUNY board. With inherited social prominence and lots of money, Beth was praised at home and abroad as a heroine, presiding over countless philanthropic and government-funded "do-good" organizations. My basic civics lessons had always taught that we Americans did not have a caste system—or did we?

Another contretemps dealt with my accompanying Clif as he fulfilled his commitment to visit all sixty-four campuses in his first year as chancellor. During one of our early visits to a community college, my tour was interrupted by a summons to the president's office. Alone together, he graciously offered me a seat, then pointedly inquired, "Why are you here?"

I explained that it was at my husband's request that I accompany him while he made his initial visits to the various university campuses. Furthermore, I believed it important to educate myself in the totality of the SUNY system.

The president responded, "Dolores, I read you as too intelligent and too professionally engaged to spend your time looking at student art classes around the SUNY system. Are you here perhaps to spy on us?"

My unspoken reaction: *Egad! I can't win!* Thereafter, I limited my visits to those hosts who sent specific invitations to receive me on their campuses.

My next little rumble with Beth Moore was over the completion of our South Tower residence. The buzz around SUNY Central was that architecturally the design was quite modern, even groundbreaking—a totally different style of residence compared to other SUNY-provided homes. The furnishings for the apartment were yet to be selected when Beth telephoned me to advise, "Jeanne Thayer has offered to preside over decorating the Tower." (Jeanne was a SUNY trustee and wife of Walter Thayer, president of the *New York Herald Tribune*.) Momentary silence was my immediate response. After all, it was I who met the challenge of locating a decent home by identifying the South Tower at SUNY headquarters as the chancellor's residence.

Beth filled my pause with, "Dolores, Jeanne is so special."

With all the resolve I could muster, I firmly replied, "Beth, I am special, too."

My husband suggested that we just continue quietly with my decorating plans, which I had envisioned soon after identifying the South Tower as a possible home for Clif and me. Once they were completed, we were eager to receive the university's trustees as our first guests. Curiously, neither Clif nor I can recall Beth's ever accepting our invitations to visit. As for Jeanne Thayer, I surmised that she was embarrassed by the insinuation that she was more suited than I to decorate our new home. Soon after leaving the SUNY board, she donated a valuable group of Frederic Church prints to be hung in a SUNY reception space of the headquarters' main floor. Jeanne asked me to assist her in the framing and installation of the new graphics. Working with my friend Norman Rice, retired director of the Albany Institute of History and Art, we hung the art in the lobby of the SUNY headquarters, creating a most welcoming lounge for visitors awaiting appointments with the officials of SUNY Central.

Step by step, I managed to put my fractured Humpty Dumpty beginning with the State University all together, eventually making a personal turnaround. Clif's career at SUNY, its trustees, sixty-four presidents, and political provocateurs had fallen neatly into place. Happily, my own team of supporters made life in the South Tower a complete delight. Maggie Clairmont, operations manager for the entire building, administered a splendid housekeeping staff for our residence; a call to her office brought

Mary Horner, our invincible executive assistant, who for eight years kept both Clif and me in orbit and back again to our respective SUNY offices.

immediate and commanding response for any and all of our needs. Then there were the courteous and professional drivers assigned to move us about the state. But the most essential contributor to my entire universe was Mary Horner, the executive assistant who handled Clif's and my travel. My peripatetic life would have been impossible without the efficiency of the professional people who managed our complex schedules. As for my own personal engagement at SUNY, all of my activities were aimed at boosting the successful career of my adored Prince Charming.

One important outcome of Clif's campus visits was his discovery of the critical need for building stronger unity among SUNY's disparate campuses. Knowing the value of good fellowship within a university system, as his friend Clark Kerr had insightfully established within the California system, Clif believed that a more unified institution would produce a more powerful, forceful, and purposeful SUNY. I asked how I might contribute to the one-for-all-and-all-for-one incentive. A smart bet was expanding the interaction among the presidents' spouses. The perfect place to begin was at the Chancellor's Forum, the biannual convening of the trustees, SUNY presidents, and their spouses.

My initial gathering was held during a weekend retreat at the Gideon Putnam, an upscale conference center/resort in Saratoga Springs. As with the carefully conceived programs for MSU Faculty Folk, I made some inside contacts allowing me to plan an event that would bring the SUNY wives together in a stimulating and deliberative conversation.

My guest lecturer for the evening was a dynamic young scholar known for outstanding innovative research, who seemingly fulfilled my goal of engaging these First Ladies of SUNY institutions of higher education. Following the formal presentation, I was approached by one of the women, herself a practicing professional, who confided in a somewhat condescending tone, "Dolores, my dear, I use these outings as 'time-out' to relax away from the campus and my office. Generally speaking, Sweetie, we wives don't need to be organized."

I gave up the lecture approach, saying to myself, "Dolores, nice try but it flopped!"

Still wishing to contribute, I made another attempt, which to my great relief was a breakthrough. I broadened the concept by dressing up my invitations and including the whole of Clif's participating Forum members.

Beginning in 1978 I hosted a luncheon held on the second day of Clif's three-day meetings in Cooperstown's Otesaga Hotel. In addition to the spouses, my invitation included trustees, college presidents, central administration staff, SUNY award recipients—every one of them! The centerpiece of each luncheon was the presentation of a distinguished guest to address the conference. These occasions became an integral addition to the weekend.

As for the speakers, I drew upon my own bank of personal friends and colleagues out of my corporate life, the arts, and Asian studies, inviting each speaker to make a formal presentation before dessert. There were such powerful people as Kenneth Clark, social scientist, whose presentation to the Supreme Court was essential to the conclusion of the 1954 landmark decision that struck down school segregation as unconstitutional; Ambassador Phillips Talbot, president of the Asia Society; Lou Harris, the twentieth century's foremost pollster, whose political insights helped steer JFK to the presidency; Michael Straight, former vice chairman of the National Endowment for the Arts; Grace Fippinger, first woman vice president of New York Telephone; Victor Palmieri, corporate take-over specialist of troubled companies such as the Pennsylvania Central Railroad; Eleanor Sheldon, scholar and one of the first women to serve on multinational boards of directors; and Rosalynn Carter, former First Lady of the United States.

Lou Harris, USA's leading pollster and political consultant addresses one of my Chancellor's Forum Speakers Lunches. Barbara Perrin, a SUNY compatriot and loyal friend, sits at left of Harris.

Former First Lady Rosalynn Carter, my colleague on the Gannett Board of Directors, addresses one of our SUNY speakers luncheons.

Dining with President Gerald Ford and former SUNY Chancellor Alvin C. Eurich (1949-51) at the Academy for Educational Development (circa 1986)

India's Prime Minister Rajiv Gandhi in conversation with William Vanden Heuvel, U.S. Ambassador, Leonard Marks, former director USIA, and myself immersed in conversation.

These luncheons heightened communications generally, and specifically too, as the wives, becoming quite chummy, requested separate sessions in which they were the performers. Typically good fun was the headliner "Travel at Home and Abroad," in which Barbara Perrin recounted a hilarious story describing the antics of an obviously well-trained monkey ransacking their New Delhi hotel bedroom in search of American dollars as Barbara and husband Bob feigned sleeping. And furthering the presentations, Estelle Block, a travel agent, provided a number of clever space-saving hints regarding how to pack creatively when traveling through different climate zones. One of her many bright ideas was to forget about carrying a bathrobe—let your raincoat double in service.

Author James Baldwin and me
at the New York State Writers
Institute at SUNY Albany

To all around cheers, these exclusively ladies' gatherings revealed hidden irritations common to us all. When I asked a wife who had lived on her campus for over thirty years in the partner's role, "Ella, what are you going to do in retirement?" she responded firmly, "I am not going to smile at anyone I don't like!"

Reflecting back upon those early years beginning with "We wives don't need to be organized," I was pleased to have pulled deep within my personal bag of tricks in the service of a more inspired symbiosis among the participants attending the Chancellor's Forum. Furthermore, it is gratifying that I was able to implement my initiatives at no expense to SUNY, as I made personal monetary contributions to the university out of my corporate income to cover the costs of my various ventures.

INSIDE ALBANY

Albany was a grand old American metropolis weathered by time and a preference for no-frills in the social graces and no-nonsense in civic management. Its self-image was grounded in its historic legacy and national preeminence as the capital of New York State. The society was pleasant but clannish, enterprising but reserved, intellectually alert but resolutely bland.

With both our sons in university—Bruce an undergraduate in Syracuse and young Clifton earning his masters in library science at the University of Maryland—the time had come for me to venture into the Albany community. My involvement in this new university proved less demanding than at MSU, and I welcomed invitations both locally and beyond.

Mrs. Betty Corning, wife of the longtime mayor of Albany, Erastus Corning, asked me to join her reading club. (It was more than a prestigious group of women; there was value to be found in their serious conversations as representatives of an intellectually ambitious group of local women.) Further responding to Albany's hospitality during my first year, I agreed to make commencement addresses to two women's private secondary schools, at which I urged the graduates to pursue professional careers.

I also spoke at two different Rotary Clubs, with one appearance getting me a spot on the local evening news with Chris Kapostasy (today an NBC correspondent known by her married name, Chris Jansing). Chris was covering a group of SUNY Albany students picketing my speech, which the students mistakenly labeled "A Mind is a Terrible Thing to Waste!" Angry with Clif over raising tuition, the students wrongly ascribed the "race issue" to me as a way of getting at Clif, when in fact my talk was about corporate social responsibility. Pitifully, many white people allow Black society but one subject: exclusively that on blackness! When I explained the confusion to Chris, she recognized their wrongful labeling and interviewed me on camera, providing wonderful coverage with added buildup to my corporate missionary endeavors.

With my business affiliations always being highlighted, I received a number of invitations, one of which made a crack in the proverbial glass ceiling: membership in the Albany Round Table, essentially a men's business group. Another was a nomination by the dean of Albany Law School, to be a candidate as one of the law school's trustees. I became the institution's first non-lawyer and first Black trustee. My appointment to the board of the Albany Institute of History and Art was a genuine embrace into the revered Hudson River arts community. These compliments were followed by an invitation to preside as chairman of the annual Albany Prayer Breakfast. Together the various affiliations raised my status among the local leadership, resulting in a request to participate in the Albany Tricentennial Historical Reenactment, a lavish event presented at two evening performances on the expansive stone steps of the New York State Museum at the Empire State Plaza.

"Tricentennial Nights of Imagination" was an historical skit held for two nights at Empire State Plaza as part of Albany's yearlong celebration of the 300th anniversary of its chartering as a city. I played Eleanor Roosevelt, and joining me in period costumes were: Mayor Thomas Whalen III (Henry Hudson), *Times Union* publisher Joseph T. Lyons (Dan O'Connell), Daniel Klepak (Billy Barnes), Pat Devane (Texas Guinan), Bruce Bouchard (Legs Diamond), Carole Huxley (Betsy Schuyler), and Albany Institute of History and Art Director Norman Rice (Alexander Hamilton).

As part of the city's three hundredth anniversary celebration, a script had been written highlighting Albany's historic political superstars, who were impersonated by present-day Capital City personalities. I was chosen to portray Eleanor Roosevelt. My good friends at the MSU Voice Library provided me with several recordings to acquaint myself with Mrs. Roosevelt voice. I rehearsed until all but dropping dead in my efforts to approximate her cadence and sound. The performances came together quite well, a bonding experience with a number of Albany's notable men and women who quickly became back-thumping compatriots.

The next ego-popping event was seeing my name in lights on the Palace Theatre marquee, having been asked to read Aaron Copland's *Lincoln Portrait* with the Albany Symphony. I prepared for the role with a friend and professional voice coach with the Empire State Youth Theater Institute. Some eighteen lines into the lyrics I read in my deepest, most serious voice: "As our case is new, so we must think anew and act anew . . . then we shall save our country."

It was here that a mental image of our adored, so very tall son, Clifton 3rd, flipped into focus, as I read with joyful pride and assured deliberation, "He stood six feet four inches tall!" The orchestra underscored my emotion with a huge crescendo!

I continued, offering my own interpretation of the script through to the conclusion, upon which the audience's applause was resounding. I rejoiced inwardly when to my ultimate delight Maestro Julius Hegyi, the Albany Symphony's beloved conductor, approached me backstage saying, "I have conducted the *Lincoln Portrait* many times, but never before have I heard it read as you have. Congratulations!" I was euphoric.

There were several women whose friendships offered the grace of a sincere welcome to Albany. Two of them, Shirley Gordon and Patricia Ballard, both professional lobbyists and wives of men in Clif's inner circle, became everlasting great pals. These expertly seasoned women took me under their wings when they attended the governor's annual State of the State address to the Senate and the Assembly. The power-packed event revealed the dynamic interaction among the Capitol's political players. The fretting and strutting upon the stage by the legislators and their aides demonstrated the ultimate in swaggering political showmanship. I was dazzled by the interplay between these elected state leaders as they jockeyed to see and be seen.

Rotary—Albany

SUNY—Binghamton

AKA Sorority—East Lansing

Another SUNY

SUNY—Hudson
Valley Community
College

SUNY—Delhi

My installation as trustee of SUNY Fashion Institute of Technology with President Marvin Feldman and Chairman Pete Scotese

We were cheerfully grounded socially with the five families Clif had recruited to come along with us from MSU to SUNY. Our Thanksgiving table could have been labeled gatherings of "MSU East." We also came to adore many from within the huge SUNY family. The indispensable Murray Block, deputy chancellor and long-time academic stalwart, together with his wife Estelle, who was endowed with the world's most delightful sense of humor, welcomed us into their home which seemingly embraced the whole of the SUNY nation. Murray, a devotee of Chinese cuisine since being stationed there in World War II, entertained hundreds, and certainly us, with his extraordinary voyages into the refined culinary arts of East Asia. We found our social interaction throughout our SUNY years to be a cornucopia of varied, marvelous friendships.

Beyond my Albany involvements were other institutional memberships that kept me perpetually on the go. The Board of Governors of the Massachusetts Institute of Technology was outstanding among my not-for-profit affiliations. Each Governor was assigned a university department or school to monitor. Mine was The Media Lab founded by Nicholas Negroponte and former MIT President Jerry Weisner. There I witnessed a supercharged academic environment that encouraged and supported advanced technological creativity.

Other nonprofits were Tulane University's Board of Visitors, which was regularly updated in the university's pioneering scientific research. Then there was the Manhattan-based SUNY Fashion Institute Of Technology, led by President Marvin Feldman, whose extraordinary vision inspired

FIT's enduring dynamism and engagement, moving through to today's gifted President, Joyce Brown.

Furthermore, my corporate life continued apace. Allen Neuharth, recently appointed CEO of media conglomerate Gannett Company, invited me to lunch and flew into Albany from Rochester, where Gannett was then headquartered. Previous experience had proven that an invitation to lunch with a chief executive was the first salvo to a board membership invitation. And so it was. I joined the Gannett Board of Directors in 1979. Once again, I was a company's first woman and first Black director.

My nine years in Albany required me to hone a different set of skills than those I had sharpened at Michigan State. While I still played a supportive role at SUNY, there were no students for me to call my own. The chancellorship was the administrative body for a campus system in which each of the presidents was in charge of his own student body. In lieu of my former interaction with students, I reached out into various parts of Albany's nonprofit community as an activist citizen.

A PRIVATE FOUNDATION

In addition, and most meaningfully, I took this opportunity to create my own private operating foundation, The Fund for Corporate Initiatives (which I describe in depth in Chapter 9). With FCI, I engaged even more deeply with the local business community. I did so by inviting a number of public companies to participate in a unique program I designed to engage business students from all the local colleges and universities. This broader expansion of my ventures facilitated meaningful growth independent of SUNY while also contributing to the expansive image of Clif's administration.

There were three corporate leaders in Albany who called upon me to serve on their boards of directors. Lewis Golub, leader of the Golub Corporation that owned Price Chopper Supermarkets, and Victor Riley, CEO of Key Bank Inc. (now a subsidiary of KeyCorp), were attracted by my FCI goal to provide groups of students meaningful exposure to corporate life in order to get one step ahead of white males by the time they graduated. Given this civic initiative and my other credentials, these local leaders believed I could make a contribution to their boards. Furthermore, these two leaders had the depth of sensitivity and strength of intelligence to see the need for corporate structural change.

A third local chieftain was James Conway, founder of AYCO corporation. Jim knew of my longtime business experience, as he handled Clif's and my fiscal portfolios in AYCO. He asked if I would become one of eight investors to establish a niche bank to serve the Capital Region. I was fairly well schooled in the banking industry, having served several years on the Michigan National Bank's Lansing board. However, I had never before taken part in a start-up business which was without doubt more personally engaging. My acuity and longevity of affiliations with the major companies convinced Conway to include me in this promising financial adventure.

The three affiliations were each in their own way different from the world of Big Business that had been my base. My primary incentive for accepting these small local boards was to show a deeper commitment to the Albany community where Clif and I now lived a good and productive life.

Upon our departure from Albany in 1987, an exhilarating honor was the Albany City Council's reception at City Hall for Clif and me. Mayor Tom Whalen and the other members of the City Council were on hand to present us with a signed copy of the Kodak Company's spectacular photograph of Albany's skyline at night—clearly showing SUNY Plaza and our tower—which previously had been projected on a gigantic screen in Manhattan's Grand Central Station. The inscription read: "To Clif and Dolores, With Thanks for Your Helping to Make Albany a 'World Class' City 1-27-87." It was a lovely bookend to my topsy-turvy arrival into what became our beloved SUNY and Albany families.

At the conclusion of Clif's tenure the SUNY Board of Trustees honored us with a splendid dinner party of some nine hundred guests from the university community and the Albany leadership. The grand surprise of the evening was the announcement by Donald Blinken (then SUNY board chairman) that the building which housed the Rockefeller Institute of Government, a public policy think tank that Clif had founded several years earlier, would henceforth bear our names.

But prior to Don Blinken's announcement was the tribute to me by Vice Chairman Judith Moyers. Judith shared with the audience a litany of plaudits in my name that she presented in poetic prose. Bearing the grace of the vice chairman's authority, she silenced the room as she detailed the essentials of my contributions in the Wharton years. Judith Moyer's fervent commendation has allowed me recall of a life in Albany well lived and well received.

CHAPTER 9

Corporate Boards

PHILLIPS PETROLEUM

"Phillips Petroleum Agrees to Change in Reply to Suit; Rearranges Board to Settle Stockholder Action on Gifts—Nixon's Personal Acceptance of $50,000 Is Disclosed," trumpeted a February 1976 *New York Times* headline.[1] My eyes popped wide open in amazement, as this time it was *my* name—not Clif's—in a *New York Times* front-page, above-the-fold business article. The story recounted a lawsuit by the Center for Law in the Public Interest, accusing Phillips of making illegal contributions to Richard Nixon's 1972 presidential re-election campaign.

The class-action suit was settled and approved by a federal judge, who ordered that the Phillips board be expanded to seventeen individuals by adding six outside, independent directors jointly approved by the center and Phillips. It was stipulated that at least one appointee should be a woman and at least one be Black. Of course being both, I represented for Phillips a two-fer, a role that was not unfamiliar to me. Nevertheless, being acknowledged in a breaking New York Times news story about this landmark appointment came as a bit of a shock.

In the late 1960s two major social and corporate issues were building to a fever pitch, both in the streets and in corporate boardrooms around the nation: Equal rights for Blacks and equal opportunity for women.

---

1   Henry Weinstein, "Phillips Petroleum Agrees to Change in Reply to Suit," Special, *New York Times*, February 19, 1976, p. 1.

Each sector was demanding full participation in business and government. Equally important, some men of wide-ranging intelligence were awakening to the realization that the time had come to deal seriously and honestly with social inequities. I was fortunate enough to have been introduced to a small group of principled businessmen who were willing to take action on the issues that would spur progress and improve business practices. Recruiting women and Blacks to the rolls of corporate directorships was a major step under consideration. Identifying individuals who could be easily assimilated into their boys club was the latest challenge of conscience.

Historically, board seats were filled with CEOs, COOs, and presidents of Big Business—nearly all of them white males. There were precious few well-established Blacks and women in such positions whom the voting shareholders would recognize to fill the corporate seats. Consequently, the names being reviewed by companies' nominating committees were well-known women and Blacks in academe and the nonprofit world, or were prominent corporate lawyers or former political superstars. In 1969, Clif was second of the first three Black men identified as outside corporate directors in Big Business. Among the female pioneers at that time were Eleanor Sheldon, president of the Social Science Research Council; Marian Heiskell, family-owner of The New York Times Company; Hanna Gray, provost of Yale University; Barbara Scott Preiskel and Kathy Wriston, both distinguished lawyers; Martha Griffiths, former Michigan congresswoman; Anne Armstrong, former U.S. ambassador to the Court of St. James's; and Juanita Kreps, former U.S. secretary of commerce.

Interest in my candidacy for corporate board membership began in 1974 with Michigan Bell Telephone Company and Michigan National Bank, followed by the Kellogg Company in 1976. Until then, my board invitations had been limited to not-for-profit groups. My earliest exposure to a corporate environment was growing up around a family business, Duncan Brothers, but the funeral home never inspired any thought of involvement on my part. However, as a Black woman I found the invitations to participate in the world of Big Business inspiring, challenging, and irresistible.

My emergence as a desirable candidate for a place at these exclusive board room tables was an unanticipated consequence of my frequent speaking appearances, two appointments by a state governor,

I am seated in the first row of the Phillips Petroleum Board of Directors (July 1991). My fellow board members included: (first row, seated next to me) Pete Silas, Phillips chairman and CEO,; (first row, far right) Melvin Laird, congressman and former secretary of defense; (second row, far right) James Edward, former governor of South Carolina and secretary of energy; (third row, first on left) Robert Froehike, former chairman, Equitable Life Assurance Society; (third row, second from left) Norman Augustine, chairman and CEO, Martin Marietta; (third row, fourth from left) "Spike" Beitzel, senior vice president, IBM; (third row, fifth from left) Doug Kenna, chairman and CEO, Carrier Corporation.

membership on several prestigious not-for-profit boards, and my breadth of international experience, including being a published author. Print and TV news coverage had added to my visibility—and, most importantly, having become a known quantity. During the era of serious student demonstrations, I was frequently seen on Michigan TV, standing beside Clif and sometimes alone, confronting anti-war protesters and calming tensions.

And yet my nomination to the Phillips Petroleum board was sheer happenstance. Martha Ordway, a great Michigan friend whose husband, Phil, was a prosperous manufacturer of plumbing supplies, asked me to join her at the dedication of a Mormon-funded student dormitory near the western edge of the MSU campus. The Ordway's connection to the Mormons was through marriage—their older daughter had wed into a prominent Mormon banking family, the Stoddards. The Ordways and Stoddards had been exceptionally gracious in reaching out to us soon after our arrival in East Lansing. Despite the Mormon Church's opposition to Black membership—soon to be lifted—the issue was never broached by the Stoddards or us. We believed it unnecessary to stoke a dying fire. When the Ordways and I arrived at the site, an official of this Mormon event asked me if I, the only member of MSU's senior circle present, would offer a few words of welcome to the assemblage. My experience in speaking extemporaneously had prepared me well for occasions like this; I was quite at ease in greeting the small, prestigious gathering.

Bob and Peggy Sears, also Mormons, had flown into Lansing for the ceremony. Most relevant to this story, Bob was a vice president and board member of the Phillips Petroleum Company. Years later, he delighted in recalling that he'd returned to Phillips headquarters and announced, in an explosive voice, "I think I've found her!"—that is, the two-fer who would meet the requirement for a Black and a woman board director, thereby allowing the lawsuit to come to closure.

Another surprising coincidence was a connection between me and the Center for Law in the Public Interest, which was tasked with approving the new Phillips outside directors. Many years earlier, one of the Center's board members, who was living in Kuala Lumpur at the same time as we were, had seen a letter-to-the-editor I had written to the *Straits Times*, objecting to the paper's coverage of a minstrel show with white Englishmen clowning in blackface. I thought it brazenly racist and said so, concluding my letter with: "Release us of this Black Man's burden." The Center board member recalled my positive tone of aggression and gave me a nod of approval when my name surfaced regarding the Phillips' settlement.

Accepting the appointment wasn't so simple for me, however. Clif was concerned about how my involvement with Big Oil would be viewed by anti–Big Business students at MSU and by the *State News*, the student newspaper, which appeared on every legislator's desk when they were in session. Clif and I met with his key adviser, Bob Perrin, to discuss my invitation to join the Phillips board and the issues it might cause us at the university. Together we concluded that any dust-up on campus would be short-lived, so my two advisors said, "OK, Dolores, go for it!"

BARTLESVILLE

Raising the opening curtain for the new outside directors upon our arrival at Phillips Petroleum headquarters in Bartlesville was not exactly a Rodgers & Hammerstein production, but it surely was Oklahoma at its most welcoming. The company's four planes were sent across the country to bring us and our spouses into the small company town. As Forbes magazine had once put it, "Bartlesville is Phillips and Phillips is Bartlesville."[2] We were housed in the company suite—an exquisitely appointed apartment on top of one of the two headquarters buildings. Even the powder-room hand towels felt as if woven of pure silk.

For the inaugural dinner party, the wives of the company officers were, to a lady, decked out in the latest designer floor-length dresses, with glamorous hairdos, each offering us sweet words of hospitable cordiality. However, the officers of the company displayed atypical reserve and a bit of incredulity to find strangers now in control of their revered company. The contingent of dinner waitstaff arrived simultaneously at each table, trained to perfection as if soldiers executing military drills. A musical trio offered amplified congeniality throughout the evening—as pretty as you please.

Chairman and CEO Bill Martin presided, outwardly calm, making complimentary introductions about us new directors. But it was his wife's worrying footsteps behind him and her tempered, pained smile

2 Quoted from 1954 *Fortune* magazine in *Phillips: The First 66 Years* (Bartlesville, OK: Phillips Petroleum Co., 1983).

that gave a hint of their underlying stress—over the arrival of a very different kind of outside director who had been given enormous powers of corporate oversight.

The next morning's formal meeting was held in the boardroom, a sanctum of quiet reserve, around an imposing twenty-six-foot-long table constructed of handsome inlaid woods and flanked by oversize leather armchairs as soft as marshmallows. Affixed to the chairbacks were engraved bronze plates bearing our names. The atmosphere was one of punctilious organization requiring respectful soft voices. George Meese, secretary to the board, was the perfect company-man in charge of the realm. He ceremoniously placed in front of each of us the sacred board books (copies of which had been express-mailed to us earlier), whose content, assembly, and protection were Meese's responsibility. The Secretary personified dependability for all board members; over time became an ever-reliable friend at court.

On my first read-through, I found the book's statistical detail forbidding. But with the swiftness of mind, business acumen, and determination of several of my super-smart colleagues, some of Phillips' questionable business practices became quite evident and, for us newcomers, an unavoidable subject of consideration. The first meeting was tense, with tough exchanges between the insiders and the outsiders. After all, we, the new independent directors, were given precise control and "sweeping powers over the company's audit functions" and most critically—as with all boards—the hiring and firing of the CEO.

As one of these independent directors, I understood the need to guard my conversation outside the boardroom and not discuss our actions or policies. A key, if unwritten, dictum that reflects one's value as an independent director is, simply: When outside the boardroom, keep your mouth shut! It is a duty I have faithfully honored.

EKOFISK

The intense exchanges during our meetings soon relaxed as the old guard adjusted to us interlopers. A sense of camaraderie evolved during a field trip undertaken by the entire board and company officers to Ekofisk, the gigantic oil drilling platform twenty miles off the coast of Norway. That trip—the full board's first-ever excursion to the platform—was at my request and to fulfill my desire to experience an actual drilling platform located in the North Sea.

Discovered in 1969, Ekofisk oil field, was so huge that at its peak, its oil and gas output amounted to more than a third of Phillips' total energy production.[3] Our party, arriving from different parts of the United States, gathered in London. From there, one of the company's ocean-crossing planes took us to Stavanger, Norway, where a twenty-passenger helicopter that droned for two hours, brought us over the vast North Sea.[4]

We had left the coast of Norway two hundred miles behind, with no land in sight and only a thin, flat line where gray sky met gray-green water. Below us, the sea churned and wind gusts whipped up waves flecked with foam. In the distance, the Ekofisk flame flared as a lonely torch against the darkening clouds. The fire was burn-off of excess gas that for me served as light signaling the presence of human life (not to mention the landing dock) ahead. Upon approach, the helicopter circled to give us a close-up view of the seven-billion-dollar facility. The Ekofisk complex comprises some twenty-five drilling and production platforms. The complex structure spun out for what seemed like miles on the sea's serpentine surface, its open-air catwalks forming a vast steel latticework like a web of giant Tinkertoys. Pipes ran in a maze-like tangle from the platforms to the concrete storage tank. Multiple glass-enclosed engineering rooms with color-coded flashing lights of Star Wars intensity announced ongoing operations. Vertiginous stilts served as both support and anchor, their bases sunk seventy meters into the muddy sea floor. I was mesmerized by the enormity of the platform operation.

At any given time, about fifteen-hundred riggers and crew called Ekofisk home. In hotel-like quarters were numerous boxlike dining areas serving the men round the clock. "Pretty good food," said one of the men I was talking with. "Better be!" said another. The workers were all men whose time on the platform consisted of three shifts of fourteen days each before returning to shore. The required working day included twelve hours actually on the job. I was concerned about the amount of time the men had to endure the sometimes brutal oceanic environment.

---

3 *Phillips: The First 66 Years*, 73.
4 The following paragraphs are based upon Dolores Wharton, "Why Take the Board on the Road?" Directorship, February 1990.

Phillips' Ekofisk Platform maintains an imposing presence in the deep swells 200 hundred miles from Norway's coast. *Phillips Petroleum Photograph.*

Phillips CEO Bill Douce and I dressed in mandatory wet suits readying-up along side crewmen before boarding a 20-passenger helicopter at Stavanger, Norway, en route to the Ekofisk platform.

But then these specialists, recruited from all around the world and carefully trained, had one essential trait in common–the toughness to withstand those oft-times brutal conditions. A calm sea during our visit allowed a few off-duty workers to sit on the edge of the platform, as relaxed as tourists fishing in the Florida Keys.

The principal reason for the trip was to see repairs to the platform's weakening sea floor. Toward the end of 1984, Phillips had discovered that the seabed beneath Ekofisk was settling, apparently due to the tremendous extraction of oil and gas. Consequently, the platforms had dropped closer to sea level than when first built. To restore the margin of safety between the decks and the water, Phillips had devised a method for raising the platform by using giant floating and semi-submersible hydraulic jacks. By 1989, the enormous job had been completed, and we directors went out to inspect what three million man-hours and four-hundred-fifty-five-million dollars had produced. I was deeply impressed and couldn't help but wonder how any normal human being had the courage and desire to pursue such dangerous work.

Apart from the extraordinarily perilous environment, the Ekofisk tour had much in common with visits to countless corporate facilities of my other companies. Such on-site investigations enhanced my understanding of the expenses, management, and policy issues that we directors were asked to approve and sometimes to shut down. In my years as a director, I toured the switching stations that link our nation's telephone systems. I watched newsprint roll through the presses at Gannett printing sites in Switzerland, Hong Kong, and plants that serve many newspapers nationwide. I saw cascades of Kellogg's cereal pouring into boxes in England, Germany, Canada, and Mexico. I even sampled Eggo waffles and Mrs. Smith's pies hot out of the Lancaster, Pennsylvania, factory ovens.

But my two trips to Ekofisk remained my corporate colossus tour, catapulting my understanding of the perils of the energy industry into another dimension.

Wearing a mandatory sanitary gown and hard hat, I check out one of numerous Kellogg cereal factories in Europe.

Each Kellogg director was honored with a self-portrait emblazoned on the front of a Corn Flakes box.

Perpetually in flight: here being received by a Kellogg company official when visiting a series of European facilities.

Bill Lamothe, Chairman CEO, extends generous compliments at dinner honoring my 21 years of service as a Kellogg director...

CORPORATE TAKEOVER ATTEMPTS

I quickly learned that life as a corporate director is rarely understood by the public. The role involves decisions that can affect world economies, international financial markets, and millions of people. Directors also are the target of major lawsuits or attempts to buy out or even destroy a company.

In 1984, as Bill Douce was assuming leadership of Phillips, T. Boone Pickens, owner of the much-smaller Mesa Petroleum, attempted a take-over of the company. Not long after, a second unfriendly attempt to buy the company was launched by Carl Icahn, an investor whom Phillips characterized as a "notorious takeover entrepreneur, and greenmailer."[5] Greenmailing, not unlike blackmailing, is the practice of buying enough

5   Merrill Perlman, "Week in Business: Phillips and Carl Icahn," *New York Times*, February 10, 1985.

stock to threaten a hostile takeover and then reselling it back to the original company at above-market value.

To everyone's surprise, Phillips, the nation's eleventh largest oil company, became one of the first to be so threatened—and twice! I became immersed in meetings, conference calls, memoranda, and flights back and forth between Albany, Bartlesville, and the Park Avenue law offices of Wachtell, Lipton, Rosen & Katz—Marty Lipton's preeminent corporate firm. Lipton had a reputation as the best anti-takeover lawyer in the country. After all, he invented the so-called anti-takeover poison pill.

The three adored men in my life—Clif, Clifton 3rd, and Bruce—understood my determination to participate fully and knowledgably in board meetings. They gave me big hugs, saying, "Go get 'em, Mom!" Their supportive embrace eased my anguish at being absent during that year's Christmas celebrations. I was physically present for the Big Holy Day, but otherwise was doubled over reading studies of Wall Street evaluations and stock ownership plans, all the while cradling a telephone receiver between my right cheek and shoulder in deliberative conference calls.

The attacks by the two raiders, combined with our own calculated counterattacks, created a cat's cradle of Machiavellian maneuvers. There were stock buybacks, exchanges for bonds, legal suits (on both sides), deliberate rumor-mongering to produce short-term spikes in stock prices, identifying alternate funding sources, depositions by sharp-eyed lawyers (preceded by numerous attorneys' briefings), and so-called white knights (rescue agents to save the company). Not only was the board feverishly working to repel the intruders, the people of Bartlesville were angry as hell and determined to defeat T. Boone Pickens. For weeks, the company employees and town bystanders wore T-shirts labeling themselves "Boone Busters." The shirts were emblazoned with a red X over a ghoulish picture of Boone Pickens. The people, including ministers speaking from their pulpits, signaled their aversion to a takeover loud and clear.

Staying on top of the minute-by-minute, blow-by-blow developments of Phillips' takeover crises became my greatest preoccupation. I engaged in the process, and was deposed by Pickens's attorney in a civil suit. The lawyer, Michael Graham, was famed for breaking the spirit of witnesses under his high-pressure interrogations. After seven years in the director's seat, I had become quite savvy in assessing corporate-type personalities and judged Graham as a crafty curmudgeon posing as a good ol' boy sporting his trademark red suspenders. Graham had no doubt singled me out as a dumb, pretty Black broad he could manipulate into revealing any inadequacies of the board.

Before my testimony, I had been carefully briefed by Phillips' legal pros in fending off the deposing attorney's "gotcha" tactics. True to form, Graham played cat and mouse, posing clever questions to trick me into contradicting myself, thereby proving that Pickens's proposal to buy the company had been inappropriately dealt with by the board. For me and for each of us who testified, Graham's game plan simply could not gain traction.

Phillips general counsel, Bill Paul, later described the result of the depositions: "Graham failed to prove that we had acted improperly under Delaware Law by rejecting Pickens's offer. Moreover . . . he failed to show that we were not exercising good business judgment."

In the end, Phillips was able to remain an independent company. But in saving itself, the company was forced to sell off assets and recapitalize, converting almost half of its equity into debt securities.

BOARD MANNERS–AND MISSTEPS

Throughout my twenty-four years in the corporate world, I never experienced any sexual harassment worth mentioning. However, there was a single moment of likely intent.

One evening following a post-board meeting dinner, four of us directors were walking to our motel suites when the most egocentric director among us leaned into my ear, amorously saying, "So good of the company to have ladies on board to accompany us men." His designs were to me quite obvious. The other two directors warned him, "Don't go that way, George!" But he paid them no heed, walking swiftly behind me to my door, which I arrived at in time to slam it shut in his face.

No comment about the incident was ever made among us. However, I believed the insult deserved some sort of retaliation on my part. As a peer on the board my vote counted! I denied the offender my support of his prominent role as a corporate sage, which he had enjoyed for years. With a noteworthy voice in board deliberations, I knocked the prestigious crown off his obnoxious head, costing him a coveted board perk. Today the insult would, no doubt, be managed more openly and the consequences for such behavior would be more dire. But this was one of the countless examples showing that seats on boards of directors have multiple values.

At Phillips, Kellogg, and Gannett, conversation among directors when flying on company planes spanned from taking drink orders to back-and-forth exchanges that could fill a college syllabus. Discussions ranged across politics, stock market activity, internet technology, and even outer-space engineering (Norm Augustine, chairman and CEO of Lockheed Martin, was the one space-age engineer among us). The only topics that were off limits were any specific references to board matters. Corporate protocol generally considers it improper for a gathering of three or more directors to discuss corporate business without a company officer present.

I am also pleased to be able to say that over twenty-plus years of travel with board colleagues, I was not subjected or exposed to any racial affront nor promiscuous innuendo—that is, except for the stupidly indignant "George" offense. However, some male directors' efforts to dominate board deliberations left me silently broiling. On more than one occasion, my contribution to a discussion was simply ignored . . . that is until moments later when a male board member would repeat my freshly conceived idea—even using my exact words—eliciting instantaneous approval and sometimes applause. Fortunately, over time, with my ongoing board tenure and more frequent participation, this pattern gradually eased.

Being excluded from social occasions was another matter. Pete Estes, retired CEO of General Motors and fellow director of Kellogg Company, would stealthily round up "guys only" to join him in touring the lavish displays at the annual Detroit Auto Show. My fellow board members kept mum regarding the unofficial outing when I was in earshot. Schmoozing in the crowded aisles displaying countless versions of foreign and USA vehicles to compare their latest design features was not my cup of tea. My rejoinder? "Let the boys be boys!"

There was, however, another issue that I did take seriously: The exclusion of women from golf outings. While I didn't play golf and even turned down the opportunity to join a golf association that was seeking a woman candidate, I believed the protests demanding the same amenities as those provided men players to be well justified. A lot of important business-talk takes place on golf courses, shared only among the men playing with their little white balls on the green. But I forgave myself. I learned to choose my battles carefully, and while this was not one of mine, I was happy to see it become a major issue in the movement for women to gain parity with men. In the corporate world that included access to links as well as to corner suites.

Seasoning, grounding, breadth of experience all provide an important base for mature contributors to board dialogue. As time passed I was joined by other female board colleagues whom I respected for their depth in reasoning and skills in questioning. There were Former First Lady Rosalynn Carter on the board of directors of the Gannett Company; Ann McLaughlin, secretary of labor 1987–1989, on the Kellogg board; Carol Laise, former U.S. Ambassador to Nepal 1966-1973, and wife of Ellsworth Bunker, U.S. Ambassador to South Vietnam 1967–1973; and Meredith Brokaw, business retailer and wife of journalist Tom Brokaw. The integrity, independence, and knowledge of world affairs on the part of these women were far reaching. In our own separate capacities, I believe we were well and uniquely prepared to serve our shareholders.

A subtle and oft times aggravating issue came from some of the officers' spouses. Wives often were invited to dinners prior to board meetings. Not infrequently, a wife would see me conversing with her

My husband accompanied me on my second trip to Norway but remained on shore with spouses of Phillips officers and directors. The following Christmas, we received this photo, signed "Clif and his Harem."

husband and would leap to his side, intruding into the middle of a conversation. Did the women fear I was a seductress about to whisk their spouses off to my bedroom, or were they bristling that I, another woman and Black, had the power to affect their husbands' careers? After a while, I concluded that this was a fact of life that had to be dealt with artfully—if at all.

One counter to this problem was Clif's willingness to attend my annual stockholder meetings and even to join me on some of my overseas trips. On my second visit to Norway for Phillips, Clif gamely joined the ladies' tours. The company wives were soon charmed by my husband, eagerly including him in their activities. Later that year, one cherished Christmas card arrived from Bartlesville with a photo of Clif seated dead smack in the center, signed by the Phillips wives, "Clif and his harem, Norway."

CORPORATE LEADERSHIP: GANNETT AND *USA TODAY*

The most important function of a corporate director is the evaluation and selection of the chief executive officer. A director has multiple responsibilities, but due diligence reviewing the leadership qualities at the top of any company is a constant to be observed at all times and with an ever-inquiring and judgmental eye.

Over the course of some twenty-four years as a corporate director, I had ongoing exchanges with extraordinary leaders whose professional strengths, differences, and performance styles I came to know well. I look back on them as my stable of Triple Crown racehorses, filled with high energy and daring that allowed them to prance elegantly into the limelight. Know this, my readers: It is the leader who brands the image of the company. I'm being forthright by saying that, to a man—and one woman, Betty Alewine, president of Comsat Inc.—they were commanding corporate leaders of wide-ranging intellect and unique strength whom I greatly respected and admired.

Among the most colorful of my superstars was Allen H. Neuharth, Chairman and CEO of Gannett. His flamboyant persona was worthy of a Broadway musical. Socially, he was a generous nobleman who beguiled guests with Cristal Champagne and eloquent speeches. In business, on the other hand, Allen could be an egocentric bully. His idiosyncrasies were legendary: a wardrobe of black suits with white shirts, as consistent as a cheerleader loyal to the college colors; white limos for land transportation; an antique Royal upright typewriter, symbolic for the veteran newspaper journalist, ever present at his airplane seat; luxurious residences, including the balcony suite on the top floor of the Waldorf Astoria for his New York City home; notoriously blistering "love notes" to hapless subordinates.

But solid within Allen's innermost core was a deep commitment to correcting the wrongful plight of Blacks and women in America—corporate and otherwise, certainly in the pressroom. One day, when Allen asked me what I would like to see changed in newspapering, I responded, "Stop the press from presenting Black people as solely indigent, ignorant, miserable people and otherwise playing the fool with foulest language." And he did. *USA Today* was truly the first paper to grant us decency as respectable citizens in a functioning society–as a given and not the exception.

Madelyn Jennings, senior vice-president of personnel and a nationally recognized Human Resource professional, advised Allen in reshaping Gannett's workforce. Together their schemes were daring and brilliantly conceived. One of the most effective and noteworthy maneuvers was tying compensation of *USA Today*'s department managers to the number of minorities and women they hired on their teams, a plan that worked wonders in increasing diversity.

Gannett also was the first in industry to place significant numbers of under-represented employees in roles of authority. In March 1979, I was the first Black and first woman Allen brought aboard as an outside director. At that time, Gannett was a chain of seventy-nine newspapers and seventeen television stations, headquartered in Rochester, New York. In 1986 Allen moved Gannett headquarters to Arlington, Virginia, into a pair of tall, handsome skyscrapers, from where he introduced his newly envisioned powerhouse to the Beltway crowd across the Potomac and the world beyond. Fueled by his inherently energetic force, Allen turned a disparate group of small-town papers into a multimedia conglomerate.

Nothing better defined CEO leadership than Allen's creation of *USA Today*. He crafted the board's introduction to his model for a new national newspaper in carefully designed stages. Over a period of one year, he corralled us directors together for after-dinner gatherings prior to

Snowman's top hat by Bruce. Gannett photo.

I display one of the earliest copies of *USA Today* in front of SUNY Central's South Tower, our home for nine years.

the next morning's formal board meetings. Spouses were included by special invitation, mailed along with our board meeting materials. The warm geniality of Allen's welcome inspired a spirit of kinship, as if an extended family had been brought together to "make a plan." Such was Allen's introduction to his brainchild. At future gatherings, his presentations provided pros and cons, visuals, charts, and costs, with projected timetables for the steady growth in creating *USA Today*'s market share. But most striking in these sessions was Allen's huge enthusiasm for his vision of a national newspaper.

Rosalynn Carter, a female colleague I very much admired, and me at a Gannett Board dinner in Atlanta

At Gannett board dinner in Atlanta, president Jimmy Carter, responded to our introduction, "I know who you are. Your husband turned me down as secretary of agriculture."

The conventional wisdom among industry sages was that it would be foolhardy to launch a national paper in that failing economic climate. But Allen convinced us that the venture was feasible in spite of the daring risks. I loved receiving the sample mock-ups distributed to keep us apprised of the product as the designs progressed. Allen also passed the new creations to us for our feedback. I got a bang out of sharing the prototype models with directors on my other boards and getting their reactions to the yet-unpublished paper. On one long Phillips flight, fellow director Doug Kenna, CEO of Carrier, leaned back in his seat and carefully reviewed several of *USA Today*'s latest layouts, each section identified with a unique color heading. Holding up the financial page, headlined in red, Doug smartly volunteered, "Dolores, I'm not going to buy your paper with its financials already showing up in red ink!"

When I shared Kenna's spontaneous criticism with Allen, he said, "OK! That's why I let you directors have copies." *USA Today* financials have been headlined in green ink ever since.

Allen's vision and financial projections convinced us that the time had come. Thus, in 1982 *USA Today* went into production, with rollout plans carefully staged for major cities around the country. New York's launch was the most extravagant, being held at Radio City Music Hall. When Mayor Koch arrived on stage, he barked in mock aggravation, "When I went to bed last night, all was well and orderly in my city. Then I woke up this morning and there were thousands of *USA Today* sales racks standing on every street corner throughout Manhattan!" Allen had orchestrated the overnight delivery of the vending machines, which appeared as stunningly upright as the famous Rockettes.

Most of us at Gannett were peacock-proud of the newspaper. However, it was met with a huge outcry by critics, who blasted it unmercifully. Nevertheless, *USA Today* has survived, defining its own niche and having been the best-selling newspaper in the nation for a number of years.

Bill Kovach, former editor of *The Atlanta Journal-Constitution* and a revered figure in journalism, said, "Virtually no newspaper in the country, nor many around the world, have not been deeply affected by *USA Today* in terms of color, graphics and brevity."

In 1997, James McCartney of Knight Ridder Newspapers wrote, "*USA Today*, after fifteen years of experimentation and tons of money, has changed the landscape of American journalism. . . . *The New York Times* is edited for the nation's intellectual elite, its thinkers and policy makers. *The Wall Street Journal*, already truly national, is edited for business leaders. *USA Today* is edited for what has been called 'Middle America'—young, well-educated Americans who are on the move and care about what is going on."

Joining Clif at one of his Ford Motor Company board dinners, I asked young Bill Ford, great-grandson of company founder Henry Ford, what he thought of the new paper. Mr. Ford responded, "I read it every day. I am always in a hurry, and *USA Today* gives all the news I need to get going into my day."

The arrival of *USA Today* exemplified corporate leadership at its most visible, creative, and proactive.

CORPORATE SOCIAL RESPONSIBILITY

Preparation for my business trips always included packing selected news clippings for conversations with my flight companions. The bundle of references for CSR—corporate social responsibility—soon grew so fat that by late 1976 it deserved its own oversize briefcase. Also included were contributions by Clif, who had a passion for materials dealing with board accountability. Melvin Laird, a Phillips board collaborator on this topic, supported me in proposing a committee for social responsibility to be taken up at board level. By 1981 the company had launched the Public Policy Committee, whose brief included activities related to social responsibility. I was asked to chair the committee in 1982, serving for two terms. The committee dealt with corporate contributions to not-for-profit organizations, education, minority employment programs, environmental concerns, and safety standards. I also proposed a corporate responsibility committee for the Kellogg Company, over which I was again given the chairmanship.

The intent in establishing such committees was to identify challenging business issues, research their potential impact on our company's affairs, and then report to the full board any concerns that might affect company business practices or our corporate obligations to the local community and beyond. Diversity in the workforce was the hot topic of the time—one that we explored deeply, with regard to numbers and promotions of minorities and women. The committees also focused on corporate gifts to PACs as well as arts institutions, churches, schools, and the environment. I was proud to be considered an activist, advocating the importance of good corporate citizenship throughout the 1970s and 1980s by speaking out in board meetings and at public conferences.

Regrettably, in many companies interest in these early initiatives has fallen off, altering the definition of corporate social responsibility beyond its original intent. Granted, corporate board activity is dynamic and will inevitably change with the times. However, given my long-standing interest, I, for some time following my retirement from my boards, continued to track the annual reports of companies that had been committed to addressing social issues raised by their CSR committees. To my disappointment, the focus on hiring practices has been significantly reduced. Nevertheless these factors not only reflect the health of the companies but also are of central importance to the greater society.

There is one other dramatic change in corporate America that evolved after my time: compensation. I have been astonished to see the

Grumman Corp. CEO Jack Bierwirth and I, co-members of Gov. Mario Cuomo's Council on Fiscal and Economic Priorities, discuss corporate social responsibility at a New York legislative reception.

Clif and I preen as the first couple chosen as members of the Committee for Economic Development.

fantastic increases in salaries paid to industry officers in recent times. They are staggering! I do wonder what could possibly be the reasoning for outside directors to grant such exorbitant and previously unimaginable compensation packages to their upper management officers. I speak from significant experience, having served two terms as chairman of the Phillips compensation committee. No longer inside the boardroom, I can only guess that today's fixation over the bottom line and the constant pursuit of compensation comparisons (aided by outside consultants whose fees are directly related to the deals they negotiate) are the forces driving these huge packages. Now my only recourse is to remain as well-informed as my reading allows, and to vote accordingly; otherwise, the alternative is to simply sell my stock!

I look back on my years in corporate America as uncommonly unique. Being the first Black woman invited to serve on three multinational boards, I participated in several major sectors of our American economy as a real player. I was exposed in depth to Big Business, which provided the engines that made the world go round. I learned, I was stretched, I had the good fortune to represent thousands of shareholders who depended upon their assets invested in my public corporations. It was a tremendous privilege—especially as an American Black and a woman—to be invited to serve. It was also a grave responsibility, which I took extremely seriously.

Never during my early years had I conceived of becoming a corporate director. Such a career role was unheard of then. As it turned out, my twenty-four years of pioneering within the corporate world proved to be the most exciting and satisfying professional experience of them all.

CHAPTER 10

The Fund for Corporate Initiatives

The ideal corporate director brings a multiplicity of skills and experiences to bear on company business. While management hires executives to run a company, it is the corporate directors who hire and fire the CEO. Furthermore, the board of directors has authority to review finances and to offer guidance generally over all operations. I aspired to meet my obligation as a fully informed and capable director (or, in the case of non-profit organizations, trustee) in all my companies' many divisions. Review of personnel was a vital component.

Not surprisingly, I maintained a watchful eye over the numbers and progress of minority and women hires, always comparing them with that of their white male counterparts. At first glance, reports of my already-functioning social responsibility committees showed the total number for minority and women hires to be reasonable. On closer analysis, however, the tallies included hourly workers, thereby swelling the total and providing a mistaken impression of positive race and gender numbers. Digging deeper, I found a significant paucity of women and minorities in executive ranks. Thus, I was spurred to ask: Were the differences due to a deficiency in their education? Discrimination? Indifference? Racism? Sexism? I wanted to find out what the disqualifying factors were. And the biggest question to myself was, "So, what can I do about it?"

My scholarly husband offered his exemplary skills, assisting me in designing research questionnaires that addressed issues related to race and gender that negatively impacted the corporate culture within

American industry. My thinking was to interview key individuals and gain their perspectives about the roadblocks (years later referred to as the "glass ceiling") that seemed to stop minorities and women from advancement. Drawing from Clif's and my own Rolodexes, we assembled a list of chief executive officers and their heads of human resources we thought would be open to one-on-one discussions with me.

Notebook in hand, I called upon carefully chosen corporate colleagues to collect their insights which, when coupled with my own perceptions, became the base for my foundation, the Fund for Corporate Initiatives, Inc. The essential goal for FCI was to advance the upward mobility of minorities and women in the corporate world. I decided to create a trial approach on which to build successive programs. But first I needed to establish myself as a legal entity. Working with an Albany law firm I filed my application for 501(c)(3) not-for-profit status, which was granted by federal court on September 29, 1980. My selection of seven trustees for the FCI board relied heavily on leaders and academics drawn primarily from the Albany area, who I knew to be interested in my mission and who could contribute to its evolution.

With the general concept in place, I worked at developing FCI's structural design through brainstorming exercises with one of my board members, Jim Harkness, who was senior research editor in the SUNY Office of the Chancellor and who early on had become steadfast with the mission of FCI. His care, skills and style suffused all of our pilot brochures, statements, and formal correspondence explaining the FCI venture. Mary Horner, a secretary who handled both Clif's and my complex travel schedules and other of our SUNY activities, was the faithful constant keeping all engines running efficiently, from FCI's start up to our transition four years later to a New York City office. (I faithfully reimbursed the university for Mrs. Horner's work on FCI projects that were independent assignments and other non-SUNY hours.)

FCI INTERNSHIPS

With my operating credentials in place, I set out to create FCI's first venture, the Corporate Internship Program, which would enhance Albany-area college students enrolled in undergraduate business programs. We matched students with local companies, where they would be exposed

FCI's first group of summer interns gathered with trustees and tutors to applaud the success of the initial
ten week summer program, Albany, NY (1979)
Left to right, Back Row : #2 Jim Harkness, senior research editor in the SUNY Office of the Chancellor and FCI trustee;
#3 Isabelle Keating Savell, journalist, author, and former press secretary to Governor Nelson Rockefeller and FCI trustee;
#6 Dr. James S. Smoot, vice chancellor for employee relations and educational services at the State University of New York
and FCI trustee; #8 Professor Tom Anderson, SUNY Albany School of Business; #10 Dr. Harvey Kahalas, dean of the
School of Business at SUNY Albany and FCI trustee; #12 Joe Balfiore, theatrical director and speech specialist.

FCI Interns work session.

to corporate activities on a regular weekday schedule while receiving advanced supervision from FCI professionals on weekends. I was courteously received by the university presidents in the region who, upon hearing my quest, provided me with introductions to the deans of their business colleges. I asked the deans—always interested in urging along their brightest students' careers—to bring FCI's ten-week Internship Program to the attention of juniors and seniors looking for summer employment. The students selected for the program became the candidates for jobs that I negotiated with local businesses.

At the same time, I approached local business leaders, persuading them to employ our interns. Among my business associates were Golub Corporation, Albany International, Blue Cross Blue Shield, Gannett's *Saratogian* newspaper, Hearst's *Times Union* newspaper, State Bank of Albany, Ford Motor Company, Mechanical Technology, KeyBank, Niagara Mohawk, and General Electric. The employers agreed to give our interns meaningful work, to pay them a respectable salary, and to include them in a broad range of business activities. The company supervisors were particularly interested in our after-work seminars, a unique feature of FCI's ongoing development of our interns. Everyone responded positively to this new effort aimed at increasing the pool of minorities and women who might enter the world of business.

For weekend retreats, I had the interns bused to The Rensselaerville Institute conference center for seminars led by Harvey Kahalas, dean of the School of Business at SUNY Albany, and his associate, Professor Tom Anderson, who taught the interns about team-building, leadership, and interpersonal relations. Jim Harkness tutored the young people in writing for the business sector; Joe Balfiore, theatrical director and speech specialist, prepared the interns for formal presentations before public audiences; and I provided insights into what was expected of the individual employee in contributing to the corporate culture in assigned companies. Many CEOs accepted my invitation to dine with the interns at the conference center, followed by a fireside chat, giving the interns an opportunity to interact with corporate leaders.

Over the years, Harvey Kahalas and Tom Anderson reported back that our young people were the most popular in receiving job offers from corporate scouts recruiting on college campuses. As Harvey explained,

"The internships gave the students a significant advantage in moving swiftly into the workforce."

My investment in the Internship Program was, on a personal level, enormously gratifying. Over the course of each summer I grew to regard the interns as my very own kids. Accordingly, they responded enthusiastically to the program, living up to my ambitions for their progress.

When Clif accepted the leadership of TIAA-CREF (Teachers Insurance and Annuity Association–College Retirement Equities Fund) in 1987, taking us to New York City, it was impossible for me to continue the administration of the program from Manhattan. Given the interest and encouragement I had received from the Albany-Colonie Chamber of Commerce, I transferred the program to the Chamber. Ann Wendth, the Chamber's regional senior vice president, promptly stepped in as director of the Internship Program. Then, William Kahl, a Chamber volunteer and distingquished past president of Russell Sage College followed, continuing the program's original mission for several years to come.

THE YOUNG EXECUTIVE PROGRAM

Our move to New York City coincided with my growing perception that FCI needed to refocus its efforts more directly on minorities and women already in the corporate workforce. Fate intervened in the person of Joseph Slater, President of the Aspen Institute in Queenstown, Maryland, of which Clif and I were trustees. Joe was intrigued with our reports on the Internship Program. Seated together at a dinner meeting, he turned to me and said, "Given our mutual interest in leadership, you and we [Aspen] should talk about a joint program for young women and minorities in the business sector."

At that time, Aspen was engaged in groundbreaking research on the subject of leadership as inspired by John Gardner, head of the Carnegie Foundation for the Advancement of Teaching and founder of Common Cause. The Institute's highly regarded seminars for senior business leaders offered discussions on the values that guided their membership intellectually, ethically, and spiritually. Aspen's scholarly grounding had been established by the philosopher Mortimer Adler, known for his "Great

Books" seminars taught at the University of Chicago. Our Internship Program, focusing on young adults, suggested to Joe Slater the possibility of bringing a younger generation of business professionals into the fold of Aspen's well-established corporate membership.

We were excited by Joe Slater's suggestion and went promptly to work designing a second FCI in partnership with Aspen, called the Young Executive Program.

From the outset, we had two goals: to prepare mid-level, high-potential corporate minorities and women under age thirty for leadership at the highest levels of corporate management and policy-making, and to give corporate sponsors a unique opportunity to invest in the future of their most promising young executives. The Young Executive Program was strongly committed to including whites, Blacks, Asians, Hispanics, Native Americans, women, and men. When selecting from among the applicants, we made specific effort to include—even to seek—white males. This was at the insistence of several astute women participants, who asked, "In that white males are part of the equation of our discussions, shouldn't they be seated at the table so we can hear from them firsthand?" Ever since that observation, our programs were a fully integrated sampling of our society.

As a trustee of the Aspen Institute, I explain how an FCI Young Executive Program could contribute to Aspen's listings of provocative offerings.

DOLORES WHARTON

The Manor House (now Houghton House) of the Aspen Institute at the Wye River Conference Center, Queenstown, on Maryland's Eastern Shore, served as the meeting place for FCI's weeklong conferences. *Photo: Aspen Institute.*

Each day's activities were divided into four parts: Leadership and the Humanities Seminar, Mobility Workshop, Executive Dialogue, and Cultural Connections. All four segments presented different resource guests daily, exposing participants to an unusually rich mix of ideas, values, accomplishments, styles, and perspectives. The topics we explored ranged from Asian and African cultures to politics and government relations, to how to deal with the media, to the popular "So You Want to be a CEO?"—which was overseen, no surprise, by my husband.

Our partnership with the Aspen Institute proceeded phenomenally well. The workshops and seminars required many guest speakers, and we had access to a treasure trove of talent, which included friends, colleagues, Clif's and my fellow board members, and the Aspen Institute's prestigious membership. Virtually everyone I approached was favorably inclined to meet and talk with smart, young professional women and minorities eager to learn and grow.

The list of guests was stellar: cabinet officers, members of Congress and the Federal Reserve Board, academics, ambassadors, civil rights champions, star athletes, performing artists, composers, authors, critics, political lobbyists and consultants, journalists, institutional investors, bankers, and a long list of directors and chief executive officers of major U.S. corporations. My quest was to broaden! broaden! broaden! the perspectives and sophistication of my participants by exposing them to a wide range of professional people who could increase their understanding of the many forces that make the business world spin.

Our prominent guest speakers fulfilled their commitment to bring provocative insights from their personal perspective of corporate America. These occasions offered an opportunity that mid-level minorities and women rarely were privy to in their day-to-day work. Resource guests arrived at the Manor House (now Houghton House) just before and sometimes at the precise moment of their formal presentations, stepping briskly from limousines and even helicopters landing on the Manor House front lawn. The guests stayed for meals, and some remained overnight to speak with our young executives informally and in depth.

A lesser but valued feature of the week was the sequential seating of the participants with the guests at lunches and dinners. One participant complained he had fewer occasions to dine with the superstars than some of his colleagues, confirming that the participants relished the value of these personal social contacts. A partial list of these resource guests is a true who's who of inspirational leadership:

Vernon Jordan, former head, National Urban League, and a leading civil rights pioneer; he became a close advisor to President Bill Clinton.

Virginia Dwyer, retired vice president, finance, AT&T; she was a director and deputy chairman of the Federal Reserve Bank of New York.

Matina Horner, president, Radcliffe College; director, Neiman Marcus Group; director, Black Rock Capital Fund; she pioneered the concept "fear of success."

Anne Wexler, lobbyist; she was the first woman to head a leading lobbying firm in Washington, DC.

Carl S. Taylor, professor, Department of Sociology, Michigan State University; former MSU Presidential Fellow.

G.G. Michelson, senior vice president of R.H. Macy and Company; she was a pioneer for women executives who served on the boards of General Electric, Goodyear, and Quaker Oats.

Helen Petrauskas, vice president, Ford Motor Company; an advocate for auto safety, she was instrumental in getting airbags installed in vehicles.

Madelyn Jennings, senior vice president, Gannett Company; she served as co-chairman of the Freedom Forum, a nonpartisan foundation that promotes free press and free speech.

Rosemary McFadden, president, New York Mercantile Exchange; she was the first woman to head a major stock or commodities exchange in the U.S.

Ed Colodny, CEO, US Airways, Inc.

Masahiro Uchida, executive vice president, Mazda Motor Manufacturing.

Pam Johnson, president and publisher, *The Ithaca Journal;* she was the first Black woman to lead a general circulation newspaper in the U.S.

Juanita Kreps, former U.S. secretary of commerce under President Jimmy Carter and the first woman to hold that position.

Harold "Red" Poling, chairman and CEO, Ford Motor Company; he was a former fighter pilot in the United States Navy.

Nick Nicholas, president and COO, Time Inc.; he also served as chairman of the Advisory Board of the Columbia University Graduate School of Journalism.

Ellen Marram, president, Nabisco Biscuit Co.; she also served as a director of the Ford Motor Company and *The New York Times.*

Darwin Davis, senior vice president, Equitable Life Insurance; he was the recipient of the 2006 Lifetime Achievement Award from the Jackie Robinson Foundation.

Bobby Short, legendary pianist and cabaret entertainer; he championed Black composers of the first half of the twentieth century, including Eubie Blake, Duke Ellington, Fats Waller, and Billy Strayhorn.

Andy Brimmer, economist who was the first Black governor of the Federal Reserve System; he also served on the boards of Equitable Life, Gannett, and TIAA-CREF.

Barry Rand, president, U.S. Marketing Group at Xerox; he later served as Howard University chairman of the board and CEO of AARP.

RESOURCE GUESTS FOR YOUNG EXECUTIVE PROGRAM (YEP)

FCI resource guest Madeleine Condit, senior client partner with corporate search firm Korn Ferry, and I enthuse over her spirited exchange with Young Executive participants.

Resource guest Vernon Jordan speaks informally with several FCI Young Executive participants in the Manor House.

Legendary jazz pianist and composer Billy Taylor brought his incredible cultural depth and sensibility to the YEP participants.

Fred Wilkinson, the first Black vice president of Macy's, shares with YEP his 26 years of experience pioneering up the corporate ladder.

G.G. Michelson shares her experiences as a corporate pioneer for women executives, capturing the rapt attention of the FCI participants

Olara Otunnu, Uganda's representative to the United Nations, shared his breadth of international experience with YEP participants. With him is James Harkness, an invaluable staff contributor to FCI's program.

Author and journalist Bonnie Angelo of *Time* magazine was described by a colleague as ninety-eight pounds of pepper out of North Carolina.

Phillips Talbot, who served as U.S. ambassador to Greece and assistant secretary of state for Near Eastern and South Asian affairs, President Asia Society, shares his broad understanding of politics, philosophy, and culture with the YEP participants.

The range of experiences of Richard Parsons, who headed Dime Savings Bank and Time Warner, and Citibank, demonstrated new dimensions of Black leadership to YEP participants.

Ulric Haynes, trustee of FCI, shared his diverse experiences, from serving as U.S. ambassador to Algeria during the Iran hostage crisis to his tenure as acting president of SUNY Old Westbury to directorships with ABC Broadcasting and HSBC Bank.

Alice Young was in the first class of women graduates at Yale and one of the first Asian women to graduate from Harvard Law School. A trailblazing lawyer, she was the first minority, first woman, and youngest person to head a law office branch in New York.

Susan Berresford joined the Ford Foundation in 1970 and was elected president in 1996. Eddie Williams was the longest serving president of the Joint Center for Political and Economic Studies, which he built into the leading Black political think tank.

Rose Hayden, professor at the MSU Latin American Studies Center, brought to the FCI Fellows program her vintage perspectives on international issues and lightened the meetings with her professional piano skills.

Andy Brimmer was the first Black to serve as a governor of the Federal Reserve System. His corporate directorships included Equitable, Gannett, and TIAA-CREF

Matina Horner, former President Radcliffe College and Executive Vice President TIAA-CREF, and I exchange thoughts on leadership for women.

Tom Wyman, a leader at Nestle, Polaroid, Green Giant, and CBS, offered a unique opportunity for the young executives to explore his values and leadership style.

Frank Savage was the first Black in Citibank's international division. He has served on the boards of Alliance Capital, Bloomberg, Lockheed Martin, and Qualcomm. Randolph Bromery is a Black geologist and former chancellor of the University of Massachusetts (1971–79), being the second Black leader of a research university after my husband at MSU.

Quintessential activist journalist Chuck Stone was a national founder of the National Association of Black Journalists. A former aide to U.S. Rep. Adam Clayton Powell, he was a friend of Malcolm X and Martin Luther King. His friendship with my husband goes back to their undergraduate days when both were active in the New England Student Christian Movement.

Albert J. Wilson, vice president, chief counsel, and corporate secretary, TIAA-CREF.

Rep. Eleanor Holmes Norton, U.S. Congress for the District of Columbia; she was an organizer for the Student Nonviolent Coordinating Committee and a prominent civil rights leader.

Bob Kennedy, chairman and CEO, Union Carbide; he served on the Board of Trustees of his alma mater, Cornell University.

Richard Parsons, CEO, Dime Savings Bank of New York; he later served as chairman of Time Warner, Citigroup, and the Rockefeller Foundation.

Arthur Ashe, tennis champion and first Black man to win the U.S. Open (1968) and Wimbledon (1975).

Kitty Carlisle Hart, singer, actress, and spokeswoman for the arts; she served 20 years on the New York State Council of the Arts and received the National Medal of Arts from President George H.W. Bush in 1991.

The Young Executive Program required intensive preparation. Several months before each program, Clif and I met with resource guests—fourteen to fifteen for each program—to discuss the goals and elicit their thoughts about how their unit might contribute most appropriately. We used these advance meetings to integrate each segment of the program to achieve the greatest impact upon the participants. To maximize their experience, we mailed binders to them three weeks before their arrival at the Aspen Institute. The packages included resumes and background readings, as well as papers and speeches by our guest presenters. These were time-consuming readings, but the collections were critical to maximizing the YEP experience.

By the end of the weeklong program, the participants began to accept as normal the appearances of celebrity resource guests. However, our young people never took for granted those rich, insightful conversations. They accepted the assertion that in-depth experience and heightened exposure is essential before being able to arrive comfortably into a sophisticated environment. Our exposure allowed them to prepare through participating in real situations and with many executives in America's corporate leadership.

Critical to the participants' experience was their residency at Aspen's Wye Plantation, set along the Wye River on nine hundred acres of farmland, woods, and creeks. The bucolic setting engaged the

Harvey Kahalas, Dean SUNY Albany College of Business and FCI Trustee, talking with three young executives.

Eleanor Sheldon, (front row, first chair on left), FCI trustee and leader of FCI's Mobility Workshops Program, was one of the nation's earliest women directors, serving on the boards of Exxon, H.J. Heinz, Equitable Life, the Rockefeller Foundation, and Rand Corporation.

I rush back to the YEP conference at the Aspen Institute via a Gannett helicopter following an unexpected meeting at Gannett headquarters in Washington, DC

participants' spirits with its soft sweet air and expansive green fields. A favorite luxury was watching the great herd of black Angus cattle grazing and sometimes staring back at us, as though we were the curiosity. Morning exercise with administrative coordinator and aerobics trainer Charlene Costello became a welcome part of the daily routine. This supremely harmonious setting allowed the young minds to shift away from corporate office ritual and to concentrate on messages developed specifically for them by the many commanding resource speakers.

By bringing together seasoned leaders and younger aspirants from multiple business sectors, the Young Executive Program provided the opportunity for communication and learning of a kind and quality few corporate professionals experience until well into their careers. Based upon their immersion in the program, we believe participants were in a stronger position to move up to and through the glass ceiling.

No final study or evaluation has been done to determine the success of the Young Executive Program,[1] so it would be naive and presumptuous to ascribe the success or failures of these young participants to a one-week, intensive course. But their individual reactions and comments are a telling testimony to the importance of the FCI experience. Some comments by three of the participants provide insight into the experience:

1   Patricia O'Toole, *Refining the Fine*, FCI Report, Summer 1996

"The normal executive programs (A) do not generally introduce people at our age to these sets of issues and (B) do not generally introduce young executives of color to these issues. And so, without this particular program most of us would not think about being a CEO, would not think about considering issues that affect boards of directors." —*Winston Smith, Contingency Planning Director, AT&T*

"You gain a perspective of the diverse issues that you need to be aware of and to recognize that these have a role in your further development."—*YEP participant*

"After nearly thirty-five years with Kellogg, I will be retiring at the end of the year. I want to thank you for your coaching and mentoring while on the Board and your recommendation that I participate in Aspen. I recall your push for Kellogg to participate, and it seems for all of us who did, our horizons expanded. I basically grew up in corporate America under your tutelage. Thank you for your guidance and unwavering support!" —*Celeste A. Clark, senior vice president, Kellogg Co., and elected in 2011 to Kellogg Foundation Board of Trustees*

I have many lasting memories attesting to the broad value of the experience. One is of Darwin Davis of Equitable Life giving insightful advice on upward mobility:

"If your colleagues are making a circle, be sure to get yourself included inside that circle." And, "If it is to be, it is up to me." Then there was the startling, candid story by Bob Kennedy, who described the ethical and moral imperatives that motivated his actions as Union Carbide CEO when the company faced the 1984 Bhopal crisis in India, which killed eight thousand people. Another is of the reaction to lobbyist Anne Wexler, meticulously studying in advance the legislative agenda of the employers of all the participants, who were stunned when she listed each of their company's legislative issues under review by Congress. There was an eminently discerning conversation about socioeconomic dilemmas, inspired by the legendary leader and corporate director Vernon Jordan, who discussed "The Outside Director: Buying In or Selling Out?" These are but a small sample of the rich fare to which our young executives were exposed.

Validation of the Young Executive Program was made clear through the participants' own efforts in networking as they conversed informally for months following their time at Aspen. Incidental conversation revealed that the "FCI alumni" frequently met for lunches, exchanged emails, and forwarded readings on managing diversity, currency issues, the changing global workforce, compensation/insurance packaging, you name it. Their self-generated post-program activities revealed that there were ongoing interests being explored by these minorities in the workplace. My reaction was that herein lay an incentive to create another initiative under the FCI umbrella.

Excited by the idea, I received my board's approval for what became our third initiative, the FCI Fellows Program for alumni of the Young Executive Program. Additional funding was needed, and it was with great gratitude that I thanked four foundations for stepping up: The Ford Foundation, The Gordon and Llura Gund Foundation, The Kellogg Foundation, and The Andrew W. Mellon Foundation.

FCI's new initiative brought together participants from previous sessions to take part in advanced seminars dedicated to expanding professional networks and sharing career insights connected with global issues of critical importance. The sessions were chaired by the Fellows themselves, who also served as speakers. I served as chief administrative officer. The Fellows paid for their own travel to designated out-of-town hotels. Then FCI took on the responsibility for all living costs related to the participants' hotel accommodations and on-site transportation.

Drawing from several editions of the FCI newsletter, "Out of the Cave,"[2] edited by Fellow Lynn Rossano, I have summarized what happened when a total of forty FCI Fellows came together during several meetings during 1994 and 1995.

The first in the series of conferences took place at Aspen's Wye River Conference Center, with twenty Fellows focusing on the North American

2 "Out of the Cave," FCI Quarterly Newsletter, vol. 1, no. 1 (Summer 1994); vol. 1, no. 2 (Winter 1994); and vol. 2 no. 2 (Winter 1995).

Free Trade Agreement (NAFTA), which at the time was being debated in the U.S. Congress. At issue was the liberalization of trade between the United States, Canada, and Mexico. Our sessions, chaired by the Fellows, included several guest speakers, addressing such subjects as "Toward a Global Perspective: Focus On NAFTA." David Hopper, chair of Ontario Hydro International and former vice president for policy and research at the World Bank, offered a Canadian and global perspective, and Susan Kaufman Purcell of the Americas Society underscored Mexico's profound political shift away from anti-Americanism and toward liberal economic reform.

Another exciting unit was led by Rose Hayden, former professor at MSU and former deputy director for the Peace Corps in Latin America and the Caribbean. With customary intellectual acumen, erudition, and wit, Rose wrote and directed a simulation, "NAFTA: Do We Hafta? Or Singin' the NAFTA Blues." Prepped with selected readings, the Fellows performed vigorously in a mock Congressional hearing and learned more about how companies and special interest groups were organized.

CENTER FOR STRATEGIC AND INTERNATIONAL STUDIES

One of my principal not-for-profit board memberships was the Center for Strategic and International Studies. CSIS is a Washington-based nonpartisan think tank dedicated to providing leaders with strategic insights and policy solutions to emerging global issues and to advancing understanding in the areas of international economics, politics, security, and business.

At the invitation of John Hamre, President and CEO of CSIS, an internationalist with extensive background on the world-stage has received multiple policy-making appointments including Deputy Secretary of Defense, generously opened the CSIS doors to our FCI Fellows. We were hosted at a pair of two-day conferences that were designed specifically to expose the Fellows to compromising international simulations.

The first was held in October 1994 at the 1600 K Street offices, another the following May. Both exercises were created and directed by the super-brilliant CSIS scholar Erik Peterson, vice president and director of studies. An example from one of his seminars began with Erik laying

Frank Carlucci,
Chairman of the
Carlyle Group and
former Secretary
of Defense speaks
"off the record"
with Fellows at CSIS
headquarters.

out this problem: "Suppose you are an executive of an American communications company interested in doing business in China. You are in Beijing, struggling through complex negotiations with Chinese bureaucracy, when you receive a message: The American government is threatening sanctions against China for violating intellectual property rights. Now what?" Then, throughout the course of the simulation, Erik continued to add additional drama and anxiety to his realistic scenario, leading our twenty-six Fellows into an exploration of international and cross-cultural problems.

Our second CSIS conference featured Frank Carlucci, secretary of defense in the Reagan administration and chairman of the Carlyle Group, as our keynote speaker. He shared his insights on Pentagon downsizing, major world tensions, and the impact of technology on America's competitive position. Noting that the United States remains the world's largest economy and has grown more competitive, he expressed concern over a potential void in human talent and for cultural sensitivity in doing business overseas, which had been overshadowed by what he termed an "order-book mentality." He lamented an absence of visionary leaders and the xenophobia that often arises during election campaigns.

Among the featured activities of these two CSIS conferences were field trips drawn from Clif's and my other valued contacts. We visited

Fellows visit the British Embassy.

FCI Fellows visit the U. S. Congress in Washington, DC

Sen. Daniel Patrick Moynihan's office and gained valuable insights from his assistant, Francis Creighton; we stopped off to tour the House Chamber; and we were received for afternoon tea at the residence of His Excellency Sir Robin Renwick, British ambassador to the United States.

A highlight of the conferences were presentations by the Fellows themselves. A sampling of these sessions includes:

Lynn Rossano discussing advances in business technology in a seminar titled "The Future of Telecommunications: An Alternate View"
Judith Kirkland, director of advanced projects, NYNEX Mobile Communications, discussing how technological advances, such as combined telephone and TV monitors and "smart cards" containing vast amounts of information, could serve American executives

Keith Rauschenbach, second vice president for Counseling/Participant Services, TIAA-CREF, explaining that though few applications other than catalogue operations were then available on the Internet, this was an evolutionary process and privacy and security issues would continue to be major concerns for corporations as more operations went online

Given the Fellows' keen involvement in this successful program, the FCI board invited several to join its ranks—first Winston Smith of AT&T and Chris Giordano of TIAA-CREF. They were soon followed by Donovan Gordon of Black Enterprise Television. The Fellows Program had become a significant part of FCI.

COMMITTEE FOR ECONOMIC DEVELOPMENT

Another prominent board affiliation of both Clif's and mine was the Committee for Economic Development (CED), an independent, nonpartisan organization of over two hundred business and education leaders dedicated to policy research on major economic and social issues. With the collaboration of its president, Charles Kolb, we held a "Dialogue on Diversity" on May 19, 1999, involving the FCI Fellows and the CED Trustees. Our Fellows, who debated CED's members, proved themselves to be articulate, strong professionals offering their insights, observations, and concrete suggestions on the critical issue of changing the corporate personnel profile to include more women and minorities. The session led to CED's publishing a monograph, "Dialogue on Diversity, Conducted by The Committee for Economic Development and The Fund for Corporate Initiatives," which was distributed to CED's total membership and beyond.

Once again, FCI aspired to contribute to the careers of these young women and men through intellectual and provocative interaction with stimulating professionals, instilling notable self-confidence as they moved up the corporate ladder.

Walter Isaacson, CEO of Aspen Institute, recognizes FCI's contribution to the Institute at a tree planting tribute beside the Houghton House with Fellows Josita Lundy, Lee Brathwaite, Ed Toy, Donovan Gordon, Nargis Ladha, Larry Bonnemere. Madelyn Jennings, FCI resource guest, at CRW's right—all rejoicing.

CLOSING FCI

By the turn of the century, many corporations had launched in-house programs addressing diversity and other issues specific to the needs of minorities and women. Also, several colleges of business had developed ventures similar to FCI, focusing on the development of diversity. Thus, I began to think that we were on the brink of having run our course. Equally as persuasive was my mandatory retirement at age seventy from the corporate boards of publicly-owned companies, which left me without exceptional access to the business leaders I had called upon to participate in the FCI programs.

In 2001, after twenty-one years, and having had the pleasure of teaching and learning from the two hundred young executives who participated

"I am delighted with this occasion to highlight our common cause."

The Executive Leadership Council honors Clif and me with the Lifetime Legacy Award, presented by Vernon Jordan, senior managing director of Lazard Frères & Co. (far right), and Lloyd Brown, managing director of Citigroup and a former FCI Fellow. (Washington, DC, Nov. 3, 2016)

in FCI programs, we closed the FCI books. I hope our endeavors contributed, at least modestly, to the upward mobility of minorities and women seeking careers in corporate America. Only time will determine the success of FCI. But for now, I take satisfaction in having made the effort to explore an innovative idea. In addition, I rejoice in the success of those participants who have already moved up the corporate ladder. Many have reached out, expressing their appreciation for having attended the FCI programs. Therein lay my extraordinary ROI: return on investment.

CHAPTER 11

Misadventures in Foggy Bottom

Bill Clinton had won the presidency, and we were elated. I had followed his campaign more closely than others, in part because I knew several of the players involved. Most important, Clinton's political positions were well-aligned with my own desires for social change. I voted for Clinton expecting a tidal wave of good solutions to critical, long-neglected domestic problems affecting America.

Shortly after the election, Clif was invited to Little Rock for an economic summit arranged by the president-elect. This was not surprising; with his reputation, national and international background, fluency in languages, and broad perspective gained from his personal and professional experience, Clif was frequently asked to participate in conferences and commissions. A major discussion of economic issues would be particularly appropriate. But as history shows, it was a prelude to another offer to join a presidential team.

Clif had turned down cabinet offers from presidents Carter and Reagan. Washington politics was infamous, to my thinking, with too many self-serving cooks in the political kitchen. Simply add wine, women, and cronyism to complete my long-standing impression of national politics. I always got a kick out of conversations with my politically experienced corporate buddies but never with any thought of taking part in the games.

Clinton's initial offer to Clif was as ambassador to the United Nations, a cabinet-level post. But exciting as that was, Clif felt that his particular blend of managerial and foreign affairs experience would best suit him for consideration as deputy secretary of state, which also was unfilled. It was an important position, to be sure, and his qualifications—indeed, his family background—made him an excellent choice for the job. After all, his father had spent forty years in the Foreign Service and was the nation's first Black career ambassador. Clif, himself, had served five presidents on foreign-policy assignments and had extensive economic development experience in Latin America and Southeast Asia.

I couldn't quite shake my strong negative reservation and even premonition when Clinton made the offer. In the end, of course, Clif accepted, and thus began ten months of high hopes and excitement that ultimately ended in disillusionment and departure.

My Foggy Bottom story began with a hectic, pressure cooker-like swirl that burst into action. Clinton wanted to have his top-level team in place as quickly as possible after Inauguration Day, January 20, 1993. In addition, the usual security checks and vetting had to be completed before the Senate could consider the nominations. The timetable required an abrupt termination of Clif's position as chairman and CEO of TIAA-CREF, not to mention uprooting us from our home and our respective offices in New York City while concurrently engaged in making the move to Washington, DC.

I don't want to leave the impression that I alone harbored reservations. Clif did, as well, and we discussed at length the sacrifices we'd be making. But when I shared my concerns with those acquainted with the back rooms of Washington, they argued that Clif in government would be good for the country. "We need more people with Clif's intelligence and integrity," they insisted. I know he was getting the same reaction from his own coterie of politically wise friends. But as I saw it, he had proven himself at each stage in his career—all the more reason to stay out of Foggy Bottom, as the State Department was called, and the cesspool of Washington politics. He—we—didn't need it!

During the fall of 1991 Bill Clinton was a dauntless young lion striding vigorously across the country, eager to energize us all. I first met the candidate on November 13, 1991, at the New York City home of Paul Newman and Joanne Woodward, where he came to speak to a small group of potential supporters. Clinton charged us with enthusiasm for his candidacy. I saw Governor Clinton on several later occasions in larger settings, including his debate with George Bush and Ross Perot, which was held at the Clifton and Dolores Wharton Center for Performing Arts on the MSU campus. It was exhilarating.

Once Clif decided to accept the nomination, we moved swiftly. He was summoned to Little Rock on December 22 to attend a press conference at which Clinton announced the nominations of Warren Christopher as secretary of state; Clif as deputy secretary; Les Aspin, secretary of defense; Madeleine Albright, ambassador to the United Nations; James Woolsey, director of the CIA; Anthony Lake, national security advisor; and Sandy Berger, deputy national security advisor.

I flew with Clif to Arkansas. A young Clinton aide, outfitted in what seemed to have become the popular fashion of the new administration—blue jeans, sweatshirt, and Reeboks—met us at the airport. Like a football lineman, he ran interference through the crowds to a van waiting to deliver us to the Governor's Mansion. There, the campus-like atmosphere persisted. The sitting room where Clif and I were taken for his first post-election meeting with Christopher had the feel of a well-used fraternity house. While the two talked privately, I made business calls to apologize for appointments missed because of our unexpected trip.

The press conference in Little Rock was held in a vacant space that had formerly housed a storage company. The vast, windowless room had been selected, no doubt, to accommodate the huge press corps and the many television cameras. Despite the throng of impatient spectators crowded together, the place was frigid, which contributed to the reporters' herd instincts as they clustered and chattered like a pack of wet chicks.

At the press conference, I was seated behind George Stephanopoulos, the Clinton assistant who had garnered a lot of publicity during the campaign as policy advisor and spokesperson. His youth reinforced the collegiate impression. Stephanopoulos could have passed as a smart, approachable student leader.

The announcement of Clif's nomination by the president-elect to a worldwide audience was a thrilling moment. But even in that heady atmosphere, I had a sobering thought. Past announcements of Clif's career changes always had focused on him as the central figure. Now, for the first time in twenty-three years in a leadership role, he would not be the man in charge. Even more troubling, we had heard rumors that Clif was not Warren Christopher's personal preference as deputy. How would this new situation play itself out?

Following the press conference, I was ushered behind the platform to join Clif and the others. The festive, congratulatory mood continued. I was close to Christopher for the first time, but since he was rushing off to another location, there was no opportunity to meet him. Moments later, I found myself chatting most amicably with Vice President-elect Al Gore about the National Endowment for the Arts. As a former NEA Council member, I was deeply concerned about the ferocious bullying the agency had been subjected to by Congress and the press over a few of its unpopular grants. Here was a chance to express my hope that the administration would choose a strong chairman to restore the NEA's important place in promoting the arts. "Do you want to be considered?" Gore wondered.

"No!" I proclaimed, "One member of the Wharton family in this administration is enough."

Suddenly, the president-elect was standing in front of me, his eyes red from exhaustion, his rasping voice painful to hear. He took the moment to speak with me compassionately, as if I really mattered to him. Then he told me how much he looked forward to Clif's being on his team. I was totally charmed.

The fateful commitment made, the process of security clearance began, and the multitude of complex forms requiring details of past personal history to the nth degree were dutifully completed, so the FBI could do its job prior to Clif's Senate confirmation hearings. Suddenly, however, my role as a somewhat bemused spectator in the proceedings was rudely shattered. My membership on corporate boards was challenged as a possible ethics conflict.

That Clif would resign his private sector involvements to accept a high federal position was a foregone conclusion—and completely agreeable. But would I be forced to give up my seat on the boards of Phillips Petroleum, Kellogg, and Gannett, as well? It didn't make sense that these companies would constitute a potential conflict of interest for him.

The boards meant a great deal to me beyond any professional or financial satisfaction. I was the first woman and the first Black American to be elected a director of these companies, and I believed I was a participant in one of the most significant equal-opportunity achievements of the century. During the more than two decades that Clif and I had served as corporate directors, we had scrupulously avoided sharing between us any business that might, in any fashion, violate our professional or fiduciary responsibilities or expose insider information. I saw no reason why I could not continue my work as an independent professional woman, especially as the usual government procedure in such cases would be for Clif to recuse himself when dealing with any policies that dealt specifically with my companies.

Yet, the impression I received from James H. Thessin, State Department deputy legal advisor and designated agency ethics official, was that the activities—profit and nonprofit—of every federal appointee and family member were automatically presumed to represent a conflict of interest. But I was not a federal employee and, unlike Hillary Clinton, I would have no space in the West Wing or any other government office. Why wouldn't Clif's recusal on potential conflicts be sufficient, as it had been in past similar cases?

Our longtime financial adviser, Mike Conway, was amused by two questions Thessin put to him: "What is Mrs. Wharton like?" and "Are we going to have trouble with her?" In my first telephone conversation with him, I was told that Clif was responsible for me, and that I must abide by the same rules that applied to him. Astonished, I replied that if this meant I was Clifton Wharton's "property," then we had a serious disagreement. As far as I was concerned, we Black folk had given up slavery a long time ago, and I had no intention of going back into bondage now. Thessin conceded that if I had been filing separate income tax returns and living with Clif as his mistress for the past forty-three years, I would not be subject to these provisions.

In the end, I was permitted to remain on the Kellogg and Gannett boards, but I was told I must give up Phillips. Presumably, the multinational nature of Phillips and the issue of Big Oil could somehow osmose from me to Clif, thereby tainting the national interest. Reluctantly, I agreed to the compromise, although I was incensed at the intimation that the ethics office was being generous in my case. Someday, I hope this issue of conflict-of-interest can be managed, allowing greater flexibility in addressing potential ethics concerns. There already are enough impediments to the selection of well-qualified appointees to public service, and these rigid rules further discourage their entry, especially with increasing numbers of wives and husbands pursuing independent careers. The final irony was that my place on the Phillips board was taken by Larry Eagleburger–who preceded Clif as Deputy Secretary.

Although Bill Clinton had announced his intentions, Clif's nomination could not formally be sent to the Senate until after the inauguration. Then there would have to be a hearing by the Senate Foreign Relations Committee and a vote by the full Senate before Clif could be sworn-in, granting him the right to officially report for duty. Still, the press of events denied us the luxury of sitting back

Couple know how to keep their secrets

Gannett News Service

Former Michigan State University president Clifton Wharton Jr. and his wife, Dolores, definitely know how to keep secrets from each other — especially the stuff investors from Wall Street to Main Street are dying to know.

C. Wharton . . D. Wharton

Last week, for instance, Time Inc. announced it would merge with Warner Communications Inc. to create the world's largest media and entertainment firm.

As a Time board member, Clifton Wharton was privy to the entire deal. But his wife, a longtime board member at media giant Gannett Co., didn't know anything in advance.

"Information like this is just kept quarantined," said Dolores Wharton, president of the Fund for Corporate Initiatives, a private New York-based organization that helps women and minorities in business. "You know something's going on because you see it in the press. But we know we can't discuss it."

Sometimes she can't resist teasing her husband after the news hits the streets. "Then it's kind of fun. I'll say: 'You knew something you weren't sharing with me.' "

Their lips were practically glued shut a few years ago when Gannett and Time were talking about a merger. "In retrospect, that was an amusing period," Clifton Wharton said. "She couldn't say anything to me or me to her."

Clifton Wharton was MSU president from 1970 to 1978. The university's performing arts center is named for the couple.

The Whartons, who have been married 39 years, have had front-row seats for the rebirth at Ford Motor and T. Boone Pickens' raid on Phillips Petroleum. Clifton is a Ford director and chairman of TIAA-CREF, a New York-based teacher pension fund. Dolores is a director at Kellogg Co., Golub Corp. and Phillips Petroleum.

"Keeping Secrets," *Lansing State Journal,* March 2, 1989

Clifton is sworn
in as Deputy
Secretary of State.
(Jan. 27, 1993)

and waiting for all the pieces to fall naturally into place; we had to assume that all of the official commands would be met as required. Clif resigned from TIAA-CREF, which extended his time in Washington for visiting key members of Congress and starting his State Department briefings.

The Senate hearing on January 22 went astonishingly well, with Clif receiving nothing but praise and a clearly articulated welcome to Washington from members of the committee. Jesse Helms, the conservative Republican senator from North Carolina, even acknowledged my presence in the audience, asking me to stand as he declared, "Mr. Wharton, you have outdone yourself!" I couldn't believe this from a man who had opposed civil rights and was notorious for his racially charged campaigns. But his vote in favor of Clif's appointment made complete the unanimous Senate approval, and Clif was sworn into office on January 27, 1993.

THE WATERGATE

Meanwhile, we needed a place to live. Mike Conway had advised us that buying a third home for our time in Washington did not make good financial sense. Thus, I began searching for an apartment. I was unhappy with the quality of those I saw, but I noticed that most hotels were well-maintained. We found just what we wanted, even beyond expectation, at the Watergate Hotel—a beautiful suite overlooking the Potomac River, with twenty-four-hour room service, a well-equipped gym with trainers, and two excellent dining rooms. The decision to go to the Watergate, whose name had become indelibly linked with Washington chicanery, might be seen as an omen of our fate, but living there was a true delight.

Determined to continue my professional life, I leased an office in nearby Metropolitan Square, where I could receive secretarial assistance, pursue my foundation and board activities, meet business associates, and write speeches out from under the hotel housekeepers' attention at our suite (admittedly, not exactly a hardship—though really necessary.) Already on my calendar were a commencement address at Hartwick College on leadership in a multicultural society and a speech to the Cosmopolitan Club in New York City on women in the corporate boardroom. To my thinking there was another side of the coin. I was the spouse of the deputy secretary of state. What were my responsibilities in this new role?

In Clif's past assignments, I was his partner at official dinners; hostess to the various groups coming to call at our home; a participant at meetings with students, parents, and alumni; the ribbon-cutter at countless ceremonial events; and a speaker before many audiences, large and small. At Michigan State, I also was fully involved in the planning and fund-raising campaign for the new performing arts center. Thus, the Wharton partnership was well-established, and I fully anticipated that at least some of the ceremonial and social duties required of a high-ranking State Department official would include me, as well.

The State Department offered no guidance, so I asked my predecessors about their official lives. Nancy Dickerson Whitehead and Marcia Dam, both spouses of former deputy secretaries, and Gay Vance, spouse of former Secretary of State Cyrus Vance, graciously received my calls and shared their experiences. Nancy also put me in touch with Patrick Daly, a former department protocol officer who joined me for breakfast to answer my questions.

My hour with Patrick Daly had profound meaning, though at the time I did not realize the full extent of it. The State Department's expectations of my role? "Very simple," according to Mr. Daly: "See to the care and feeding of your husband."

That was a jolt. Our life was a full partnership that Clif and I had shared for forty-three years. I pressed on. Would we be expected to extend social invitations to foreign diplomats? Mr. Daly responded, "Certainly, you wouldn't want to do anything that might embarrass the president."

Well, no, I wouldn't. If that was the State Department's expectation, I must say I resented what seemed to be an institutional reflection on my competence to move in diplomatic circles and their assumption that I was incapable of conducting myself within the guidelines of our country's foreign relations. Although Clif and I were not in government service during our years in Singapore and Malaysia, my father-in-law, the ambassador, saw to it that I received department publications on protocol for overseas posts. And hadn't the years of interacting with the international diplomatic corps in Southeast Asia and functioning in many sensitive situations since provided me with the intelligence to avoid embarrassing my country?

Of course, Mr. Daly did not know me, and I hoped he was merely reciting department policy; nevertheless, our meeting left my new role undefined. All I wanted to do was to make whatever contribution I could to my husband's official responsibilities, and thereby serve my country, too. But I could now see that my role would just have to evolve. Eventually, it did so.

In contrast to my interaction with Mr. Daly, another State Department official seemed to value my life experience. He was in charge of "prepping" wives of ambassadors before going abroad. He asked if I would speak with the women about my own initiatives as I stood beside my husband throughout his several professional careers. (It was common knowledge that many spouses felt unrequited in their foreign posts—in other words, boredom had become an issue!) I accepted the request and spoke with the women on two occasions.

The deputy secretary of state is the first person delegated to substitute for the secretary of state at official, ceremonial, or social functions, and apparently Warren Christopher's calendar was rarely free to accommodate such events. Word was that he did not do so even when serving as deputy secretary of state under Cyrus Vance in the Carter administration. Clif felt that attending diplomatic functions was relevant to the responsibilities of the State Department. Furthermore, I delighted in interacting with diplomats from around the world at a profusion of dinners and receptions, as well as hosting with Clif at gatherings in the majestic diplomatic rooms on the eighth floor of the State Department. Thus, we attended a considerable number of official events when the Christophers declined.

During my ten months in Washington, my interaction with Warren Christopher and his wife, Marie, was limited. I first met Christopher just prior to Clif's swearing-in, when we accompanied him to a State Department reception. We walked together from the secretary of state's office to his private elevator and rode from the seventh to the eighth floor. That was to be my longest one-on-one conversation with the Secretary.

We also met when Clif and I accompanied him on the drive to attend Supreme Court Justice Thurgood Marshall's memorial service, and on later occasions when standing alongside the Christophers, as the four of us shook hundreds of hands in State Department receiving lines. Such was the extent of my relationship with the man for whom my husband was to serve as chief lieutenant.

Several weeks after Mrs. Christopher had moved to Washington, I called the Secretary of State's office to ask if I might make a courtesy call on her. This was a formality Ambassador Wharton had recommended when we first went abroad. I have followed the custom ever since, as a way of paying my respects to women who ranked as "first lady" in the different communities where we have lived. In this instance, however, I was told, "Oh, Mrs. Christopher is just not into that kind of thing." I apologized for the inconvenience, explaining that I knew Mrs. Christopher only from a brief television glimpse, but now I looked forward to meeting her in person, given our mutual interest in the success of the Clinton administration.

A few weeks later, Mrs. Christopher invited me to lunch at Citronelle, a Georgetown restaurant. We had a pleasant and uncomplicated chat, but there never was much conversation beyond that, despite a genuine effort on my part. During the 1993 opening of the United Nations, Mrs. Christopher hosted a morning coffee at the Metropolitan Museum of Art for the wives of visiting foreign dignitaries. I caught the earliest morning shuttle flight from Washington to La Guardia, dashed to the Met, and arrived just in time to hear Mrs. Christopher greeting the large crowd. When most of the women left for a museum tour, I complimented Mrs. Christopher on her welcoming remarks, but her stony glare and abrupt turn in the opposite direction ended any thought of a friendly discourse. Over the years, when I have met socially with wives of Clif's associates, their general demeanor toward me often served as a barometer of their spouses' attitudes about Clif. That chilling moment with Mrs. Christopher proved to augur events to follow.

I was disappointed. I had imagined that being involved with the Clinton administration and the leadership of the State Department would be a team effort. The lack of collegiality and shared sense of excitement in support of our mission shocked me. It was another early lesson about life in official Washington, where so many political appointees seemed to have separate agendas.

Conversely, there were other aspects of the State Department's authority that were wonderfully supportive. I quickly learned to respect and trust the professionals—the men and women who had chosen careers in foreign service and were dedicated to their work. Problematic, however, were the high-ranking political appointees. Their eyes were on different targets. Some had been waiting around since the Carter administration for another bite of the apple. Others came in with a constituency behind them but little practical experience, such as members of a campaign's inner circle who had been rewarded with a high-ranking position. There were the zealots and the incompetents. Of course, not everyone fit these descriptions; many, like Clif, truly wanted to be a part of a common mission in pursuit of shared, genuinely lofty ideals.

Despite the icy reception by State's top administrator, Clif and I were graciously welcomed to Washington with wonderful dinners given by our friends of long standing. Vernon Jordan, former Secretary of Labor Ann McLaughlin, and former Secretary of Transportation William Coleman hosted beautiful and intimate gatherings. Discussions of political events were especially rich at these private parties. Washington observers, pundits, even government officials spoke with lively, non-political freedom, mindful, of course, that the guests frequently included members of the press.

FOREIGN AFFAIRS

The formal embassy parties were actual newsmakers unto themselves. Vice President and Mrs. Gore's dinner for President and Mrs. Mubarak of Egypt at Blair House was resplendent in this regard. Seated at President Mubarak's right, I saw firsthand what a strong and demanding personality controlled that country, as he held forth on how and why his government dealt with extremists, his concerns regarding his nation's place in the global community, and the status of women in Egypt. Seated on my right was Tom Foley, the Speaker of the House, who was most genial and openly willing to chat about the House of Representatives. This was Mr. Gore's first official dinner in receiving a head of state, and having carried out his welcoming remarks to perfection, he relaxed momentarily at the podium with a noticeable sigh of relief. Recognizing the reason for his instantaneous ease, every guest seated in the elegant formal dining room at Blair House applauded the charm of the man in that moment.

Many occasions resulted in cultivating strong ties among the foreign diplomatic community. Given our well-established relationships with the Southeast Asian ambassadors and their families, and briefings offered me by State Department country specialists when interacting with foreign diplomats and their spouses, I had a unique opportunity to learn and study.

During his tenure, Clif made three foreign trips, and I was privileged to accompany him on two of them. My first was to Turkey, where Clif represented the United States at the state funeral of President Turgut Özal, and the second to Southeast Asia to reinforce our strong commitment to those nations.

On April 19, 1993, we flew to Ankara, aboard a Boeing 707 that once was President Lyndon Johnson's Air Force One. (I slept overnight in the aircraft on a full-size bed!) Our entourage included former U.S. diplomats who had worked closely with the Özal government, as well as specialists on the politics and critical issues of the region.

We had barely settled in a heavily patrolled suite in our Ankara hotel when former Secretary of State James Baker asked if he and Mrs. Baker could call on us. By happenstance, the Bakers were vacationing in the region, and because the customary protocol is for a president, vice president, or secretary of state to attend the funeral of a foreign head of state, Baker had been asked to be the formal head of our U.S. delegation, with Clif as the chief State Department representative. The four of us had a delightful get-acquainted meeting, and I swooned over the Bakers' affability and genuine spontaneity. Oh, that our own Secretary could have been so accepting of us!

My regard for the Former Secretary grew the next day as we moved ceremoniously through the funeral proceedings and into the mammoth luncheon for visiting dignitaries. Mr. Baker seemed to know all the five hundred–plus guests by name, bringing many of them to meet Clif and me and encouraging contacts that could be important in Clif's work. We were awed and grateful for his generous thoughtfulness. Baker and his wife spent more time with us in that one reception than the Christophers did during our entire stay in Washington. Little wonder, then, that I hold Secretary Baker in highest esteem.

For me, the most exciting adventure of our Washington period was an official fourteen-day trip to Thailand, Cambodia, Malaysia, Singapore, Indonesia, Brunei, and the Philippines, a region that had been such a major part of our lives since 1958. The journey began with a wonderful sendoff. Early on the morning of June 17, we were greeted at Andrews Air Force Base by ambassadors from four of the countries we were scheduled to visit, along with their wives and other diplomats who had come to bid us a fruitful journey to their homelands.

Clif headed a sixteen-member team from the State Department and related agencies. His assignment was to reinforce President Clinton's commitment to full engagement in Southeast Asia at all levels—diplomatic, economic, and security—and to consult with the national leaders on a range of regional and global issues. In his meetings with prime ministers, kings, presidents, government ministers, and the press, Clif signaled that Washington was striving for a new spirit and enlarged vision in our relations with countries in the region. He was in constant contact with Secretary Christopher through daily communiques, and the responses indicated that the department was pleased with Clif's visits as they were proceeding. Certainly, the local media coverage was most positive.

The trip provided an excellent opportunity for me to catch up with old friends and associates, some of whom had assisted me in preparing my book on the contemporary artists of Malaysia. In Bangkok, Kuala Lumpur, Singapore, Bogor, and Manila, we met with Clif's former students and foundation grantees, many of whom were now in prominent positions in government, business, and academe. While we had separate schedules that did not involve me in policy discussions, I did join Clif in meetings with the American business community. Despite my twenty years of experience as a director of multinational corporations and the fact that I had met many of these same individuals on earlier business trips, the State Department only very reluctantly acceded to my presence in Clif's meetings.

I was particularly pleased to attend gatherings with professional businesswomen, enabling me to hear their opinions and to advance their ideas on the status of women and their expectations for the future. I was profoundly impressed with their insights. While their priorities tended to be different than ours in the United States, I found that we shared many of the same values.

I also was honored to be received by wives of national leaders. In Phnom Penh, Cambodia, I had an audience with Princess Monique Sihanouk, whose husband, Prince Norodom Sihanouk, was again presiding over his long-troubled country. With her soft-spoken bearing and authority, the princess was surely the influence that led her husband to change the customary separation of women when officials were visiting the palace. With a grand gesture, Prince Sihanouk ushered his wife and me into a ceremonial lounge where he was to meet with Clif, saying in an expansive tone, "Let us no longer separate the women from the men. They must join us!" Later in the year, a new constitution elevated the couple to be the nation's royal king and queen.

In Manila, where Philippine President Fidel Ramos had been in office less than a year, his wife, Amelita, took precious time to give me a personal tour of Malacañang Palace, modestly but proudly pointing to the beautiful indigenous hardwood, crafts, and Filipino art pieces. The contrast between the luxurious lifestyle of former First Lady Imelda Marcos and the unpretentious Ramos family was frequently but always discreetly alluded to. Even the door to Imelda's shoe closet, filled with conceivably one hundred pairs of shoes, was open to my observation.

The most noteworthy visit of the trip was to the oil-rich sultanate of Brunei on the northern coast of Borneo. The two wives of the Sultan—Her Majesty Raja Isteri Pengiran Anak Hajah Saleha and Her Royal Highness Pengiran Isteri Hajjah Mariam—received me in their respective palaces–prized invitations indeed . The palaces were so spectacular I thought I might have strayed into an Arabian Nights fairy tale. Both women were true to Muslim traditions in dress, covering their heads, wrists, and ankles; yet they were interesting conversationalists and refined hostesses. Her Majesty, the "number one" wife, conversed with me in Malay about the cultural heritage of the country in its dance, festivals, and foods. With Her Royal Highness, the second wife, the subject centered on the rearing and education of young children; this exchange was conducted in English.

Given the profusion of family portraits on display, it was apparent that the two women were deeply devoted to their husband and their respective children. Gossip held that their lives were totally separate from each other until the rumored courting of a third wife, at which point the two found a shared interest in the question of how best to maintain the status quo. It was an unforgettable experience, gracious in the Brunei tradition while at the same time totally otherworldly.

Near the end of the journey, I was running on pure adrenalin, with full days, short nights, and frequent six a.m. "wheels up" flight departure calls. Every minute of those two weeks had been meticulously scheduled to accommodate the meetings, lunches, dinners, press interviews, and horrendous traffic jams (many created by our own motorcades, which required police escorts) in the capital cities. We were grateful for the expertise of the personnel at our various U.S. embassies, as well as for the hospitality of the host countries that allowed us to succeed in meeting the responsibilities of that extraordinary trip to Southeast Asia.

We returned to Washington exhilarated, with a sense of "mission accomplished." Clif had every reason to believe that his diplomatic trip was a resounding success. On the department's immediate docket was a July meeting in Singapore of the Association of Southeast Asian Nations (ASEAN), which Warren Christopher would attend. Having just returned from the region, where the upcoming assembly had been an important topic of discussion among the national leaders, Clif anticipated sharing his observations in Christopher's briefings for the meeting.

I was astounded, however, when Clif was excluded from the preparations. This didn't make sense, given the just-completed mission and his past experience in the area dating back thirty-six years. During our evening walks around Washington Harbor and Georgetown, we speculated about possible reasons for the snub. Was it the cliquishness that was so manifest among the State Department leadership and the White House National Security Council staff that made him an outsider?

There was no clear answer, and Clif reminded me that he was frequently excluded from policy meetings over current hot issues, such as Bosnia, Haiti, and Somalia. I was amazed that the policy-makers were not eager to invite fresh perspectives, which was so strongly advocated in the early days when President Clinton took his cabinet to Camp David to inspire teamwork and collaboration. Had these occasions been, in retrospect, no more than lip service to an ideal not truly respected?

It was not that Clif had nothing else to do. Hardly. At the outset, Christopher had given him three main assignments: reorganization of the lugubrious State Department bureaucracy, oversight and restructuring of the government's international affairs budgets, and review and reform of the United States Agency for International Development (USAID).

All these tasks were well on schedule. In fact, the USAID report and recommendations had been completed. But Clif was only permitted to share selected findings from what became known as the Wharton Report with a few key members of Congress, where they were well-received. For whatever arcane reasons, the White House NSC staff refused to make the full report public, though eventually it served as the framework for new legislation and major efficiencies in the foreign-aid program.

So, despite our concern over Clif's exclusion, the weeks went by with no particular apprehension. Certainly, there was no hint of displeasure from Warren Christopher over Clif's performance during their meetings. They had met one-on-one daily when the secretary was in Washington.

THE RUMBLING 'SHAKE-UP'

Then the thunderous rumblings began. On October 23, I was conducting one of my FCI programs at the Aspen Institute in Queenstown, Maryland, when Clif telephoned me with an ominous warning to "Fasten your seat belt!"

He had received word that the forthcoming issue of *Newsweek* carried a paragraph in its Periscope section—a few pages devoted to high-level gossip and short items written with pretentious irreverence—headed "State Shake-Up?" It purported to describe "rumblings" in the State Department with Clif at the "epicenter" as a "university chancellor with little foreign-affairs experience . . . now regarded as prickly and unreliable." It went on to suggest that an "exasperated" Christopher "needs more help."

Of course, there was absolutely no attribution for the statements— which *The Washington Post* later would call a "slug's trail of anonymous, whispered explanations." Besides, there had been no attempt to interview Clif before the insinuations were printed. The malign intent was obvious. It was the typical Washington ploy of sending messages by using eager and gullible media as the purveyor. The "exasperated secretary needing more help" excuse was laughable, given that Christopher and his colleagues had excluded Clif from the majority of their policy discussions. But I wasn't laughing.

Hearing nothing from Christopher, Clif's immediate reaction was to seek a meeting with him. He knew that the only way to deflate such a story and maintain his own effectiveness was to have the department issue an official flat denial. Clif and Christopher met on October 28. After the meeting, my husband related to me that Christopher believed that Clif had an undefined "problem" with the White House. Secondly, Christopher added, he, himself, was not getting the foreign policy support he needed. This was astonishing, given the limitations that had been placed on the scope of Clif's assignments. The two agreed to meet again on Saturday, November 6, after Christopher returned from a family wedding in California.

In the meantime, many friends acquainted with the wiles of Washington suggested that we pay no attention to the rumors. My friend and colleague on the Gannett board, columnist Carl Rowan, recommended that we "just batten down the hatches and keep on going."

We tried, but it wasn't easy, especially after a similar item appeared on November 3 in the *Washington Times*. This said that Clif would not be fired and there was no timetable for his departure, then added: "White House officials traditionally use such leaks to signal displeasure with top appointees in hopes that they will step down." A contemptuous tradition, to my thinking!

At a State Department press briefing, spokesman Mike McCurry told questioners that he was "not aware of any truth to that item." He added, "I think the Secretary highly regards Dr. Wharton, both professionally and personally, and I'm not aware of any plans to change his status as Deputy Secretary."

His office told the media, "We would steer you away from that."

Dee Dee Myers, the president's press secretary, dismissed the question as "rumors, rumors, rumors." Then she added, "Of course, some rumors become true, even though they're not true when they start." (I was reminded of another example when Ms. Myers's own professionalism and job tenure were the subject of critical, highly placed leaks.)

In the absence of clear-cut denials from the White House, the situation was worsening. The word "scapegoat" started to appear in the press. An Albany *Times Union* editorial said: "With Mr. Christopher under intense pressure to produce some foreign policy victories, and soon, it's understandable that he's ready to shake up his department. What's incomprehensible is that the Secretary should think Mr. Wharton is one of his problems, when he clearly is one of State's best assets. Getting rid of him won't do the Secretary, or the nation, a bit of good—and it just may inflict a great deal of harm."

Clif decided that the upcoming Saturday meeting with Christopher would have to settle the matter once and for all. I made my own feelings clear, saying: "If he won't give you his support, let's get the hell out of here!"

No support was forthcoming. Although Clif had prepared a detailed plan that would have brought him more fully into the foreign-policy loop, he said it was clear that Christopher was not prepared to issue an unequivocal rebuttal to the leaks and lies but preferred that the issue—and Clif—just fade away. Clif would not accept that evasive solution. He told Christopher that he would resign immediately.

Christopher played out the game to the last card, asking if Clif were interested in another administration position, such as an ambassadorship to Great Britain's Court of St. James's. Clif declined the offer.

On Monday morning, November 8, Clif submitted his resignation. In it, he noted his initial reluctance to enter government service but said he was persuaded by the opportunity to help shape Clinton foreign policy in the post–Cold War era. "Sadly, my earlier instincts proved to be correct," he wrote. "In the past two weeks, I have found myself the target of virtually a textbook exercise in the insidious Washington practice of professional derogation by anonymous leaks."

In the closed environment of the State Department, it was impossible to dismiss the attack as mere gossip. "The fact is that working for a President is unique. One cannot simply shrug off such pernicious attacks and continue to be effective in the absence of supportive refutation of the leaks," Clif's letter continued. "Perhaps my greatest regret is not so much a personal one, but rather that the process to which I have been subjected, in the long run, damages the Presidency and government more than the individual involved. I am afraid it will contribute to a reluctance of individuals, who are willing to make personal sacrifices, to serve their government."

Off went the letter to the White House. Then, according to Clif's description of the distressing, pressure-packed day, the dark script of Washington spin-doctoring began to unfold. Almost immediately, back came a "Dear Clif" letter from Bill Clinton. In it, the president noted Clif's "outstanding service" and "important contributions." He added, "I sincerely hope I can call on you for specific assignments in the days ahead." The president even telephoned Clif to convey the same sentiments.

But in spite of the exchange, the White House was not ready to release the correspondence to the media. The objection? Clif's remark about the "absence of supportive refutation of the leaks" ruffled their sensitivities. David Gergen, the former Republican functionary and reporter who had recently joined the White House to repair the president's image, called

Clif to request that a statement, rather than the letter, be issued, sans the offending clause.

Clif said he was reluctant to accede because the lack of support from either Christopher or the president was the trigger to his decision to resign. But in the interests of concluding the unhappy episode quickly, he modified his statement and returned it to Gergen.

Still, it wasn't over. All day, the nit-picking calls continued and final clearance was delayed. As the hours passed, it became obvious that the White House was deliberately postponing the announcement until it would be too late for the evening newscasts. The network anchors would have only the bare fact of the resignation, which already had been leaked, but nothing of the content of Clif's statement. With deliberate shifts and purposeful time delays the White House had blocked Clif's factual message to the evening news hour.

It took us exactly one week following the resignation to pack out of Washington and return to our New York City apartment at United Nations Plaza. Clif's previous speech commitments were kept, and he was received everywhere as a hero returning from the wars.

RETURNING TO NEW YORK

The public response, in fact, was gratifying, if that is an appropriate word to use in this sordid affair. "Laying It Off On Clifton Wharton" was the headline on a *Washington Post* editorial, while "A Scapegoat Leaves the Team" was the message from the *Chicago Tribune*. Both remarked that Clif's departure was a cover-up for the foreign-policy failures of the State Department and National Security Council. A column by A. M. Rosenthal in *The New York Times* and letters to the editor were very supportive. We were inundated with calls and letters from friends, colleagues, and people we had not seen for years, who were appalled by what had happened.

There was the darker side, too, that seemed to put the blame on the victim. *Newsweek,* apparently pleased with the success of its prediction, published another Periscope item stating that Clif had been "forced to resign," citing his "lack of foreign policy experience." Despite the falsity of both allegations, they unfortunately became gospel for too many writers who, recklessly or lazily, repeated them in their stories of the incident. We heard that one high administration official, although not directly involved, believed that the White House had soured on Clif because he was not a team player. Of course, one must first be asked to join the team in order to play!

Because Black Americans know how insidiously prejudice lurks below the surface, I have been asked if I thought race played a part in this episode. Although columnists Rowland Evans and Robert Novak initially disparagingly dismissed the choice of Clif as a "Black" appointment, we saw no overt signs that racial discrimination was a factor then or in subsequent events. Yet, I harbor an intuitive sense that top elements of the State Department saw themselves as an elite, which made it easier to exclude Clif from their councils and ultimately to turn their backs on him. As the highest-ranking Black official in State Department history, Clif was proud to have broken new ground in the department's hierarchy, as his father had before him. But his career, indeed his life's work, had been built on accomplishment rather than the color of his skin.[1]

Am I sorry we went to Washington? Not entirely, even though the ending was ugly and painful. I relished the stimulation of the fascinating people we met in the diplomatic community, the non-government friends we made, the loyal professionals in the State Department, and—even though unofficially—the honor of being a representative of my country when I traveled beside my husband.

But I despair that people of proven ability and achievement who are willing to contribute their talents to help their country can be treated so shabbily. Unfortunately, it is all too common in Washington that their willingness to serve ends in attempts to destroy them. Most of all, thinking back to those heady days of the Little Rock announcement and the promise of the new administration, I felt I had been betrayed.

---

1   Clifton R. Wharton, Jr., *Privilege and Prejudice: The Life of a Black Pioneer* (Michigan State University Press 2015)

CHAPTER 12

Our Sons

"The boys!" So easily, so simply said, but with a reality that for me is massively significant, as if the sun were bursting forth plumes of brilliant colors suffused with the joys of spontaneous hugs, laughter, running zigzag, throwing Frisbees, twirling Hula-Hoops, shouting silly quips, fun-loving smiles—belonging to me, to us, to the moments of harmony with the four of us together—our exclusive world, embracing only us four. So brief, too brief. Alas, no more.

By the time "number-one son" Clifton R. Wharton 3rd was three, he had his own library card. He loved to read, and he loved being read to—by his mom, his dad, and sometimes his visiting grandfather, Clifton Sr. We remember his eyes widening and staring brightly into the distance as his imagination transported him through poems and stories. He would clap his hands with joy at the suggestion of going to the neighborhood library, where he selected his own books from the children's shelves. The librarian was wonderful to him; his head barely reached the top of her desk, but she treated him as a grown-up. After stamping the return-due dates inside, she handed the books back to him. Young Clifton would march smartly home, small hands clutching his newly borrowed treasures firmly to his chest.

This love of books proved to be so prominent in our little boy's life that he grew up to be a fully accredited librarian. Clifton 3rd spent sixteen years at the Enoch Pratt Free Library in Baltimore and received his MA in Library Science from the University of Maryland. He found personal gratification in reading to children's groups visiting the library. Once, while working in the Children's Services department, Clifton was

Clifton 3rd, 13, and Bruce, 6,
in Palo Alto, CA (1965)

surrounded by several obstreperous third graders. One little boy's abhorrent behavior suggested to Clifton that the child was overwhelmed by the heightened atmosphere of this stately library building. Clifton, six feet four inches tall, dropped to one knee, lowering his head until his face was inches away from the disrupting child. Then he grinned broadly saying with endearing empathy, "You know, I used to be just the same size as you!" The little guy smiled back at Clifton, quieting his rambunctious antics and settling down calmly for the remainder of the hour.

He has left us now, forever. Born in 1952, Clifton 3rd died of a brain aneurysm in 2000 at age forty-eight. I can't reach out to, or for, him any longer. He's gone, and I hurt. Oh, I do so hurt. Huge numbers of others, including young Clifton's countless associates at the Enoch Pratt libraries, hurt as well. In fact there were so many that Carla Hayden,[1] Clifton's boss and director of Enoch Pratt Libraries, closed all of the branches of Baltimore's libraries for the morning of his memorial service in the rotunda of the main library, allowing countless friends to attend. While we miss him beyond the furthest reaches of the universe, our loss is softened a bit by the Enoch Pratt Free Library's Reader Program, established in his memory. With the generous funding from many caring friends joining us, we introduced a uniquely creative reading program for grade schoolers in the inner city of Baltimore.

The Clifton R. Wharton 3rd Designated Reader Program offered, what we believed, was an imaginative approach to teaching and learning coupled with its primary objective—to expand the lives of young people through the wonders of reading. As described in its final report, "The program supplements—and strengthens—existing methods of teaching reading by bringing in theater arts graduate students as instructors to use their dramatic skills to engage and excite the children. Acting and pretending are experiences adopted as a stimulus to reading."[2]

Of the many people who contributed to the development of the Reader Program, the most central was Coordinator of Children's Services Ellen Riordan, one of Clifton 3rd's treasured colleagues. She built the team that brought the program into being. We are deeply grateful to Ellen and

1 She became the 14th Librarian of Congress on September 14, 2016.
2 E. Christine Potts, "Good Books in the Right Hands: Making a Difference—The Clifton R. Wharton 3rd Designated Reader Program," Enoch Pratt Free Public Library, Baltimore, MD.

all who worked with her. It is our profound hope that this experimental program, which Enoch Pratt operated for ten years, has worked a bit of inspiring magic for several hundred school children in Baltimore. My husband and I also harbor the thought of "a world full of children who love to read" as a memorial that Clifton would warmly smile upon.

BRUCE COMES INTO HIS OWN

"Number-two son" Bruce, born in Singapore on April 17, 1959, is an impressively self-assured adult, six foot two and male-model handsome. He earned an MBA degree from Michigan State University, and with twenty years of experience in hotel management, he is a recognized professional in the hospitality industry.

Before getting too far ahead in his story, I must quote from a letter I wrote to my mother when Bruce was ten weeks old. It speaks to my exhilaration over this wee, fist-punching babe:

> *Singapore, July 1, 1959*
>
> *Now about this baby! Bruce Duncan Wharton is the kind of baby that is portrayed by authors as exemplary, but experienced mothers know that their infants even exceed perfection. I have to pinch myself sometimes to see if I'm dreaming about this round-cheeked cherub and sometimes pinch him to see if he is real. We three are silly over every smile, yawn, and head bob our ten-week-old makes. Clif 3rd is quite proud to show off Bruce to visitors, at the same time he displays his own baby pictures so that the ooohs and aaahs are evenly distributed between himself and his brother.*
>
> *Bruce is growing and gaining like everything else in the tropics—with astonishing rapidity. He does live a considerable part of each day in an air-conditioned bedroom to avoid prickly heat. The irritation can become severe, quickly developing into impetigo. The American doctors and hospital, Seventh Day Adventist, had and still are giving us the same medical care we would have received at home. During our ten-day "internment" the Asian nurses made me feel like the Queen Sheba as I lay in my floral-filled suite. Big Clif says that Bruce looks like him. But really he doesn't. He looks like me. One thing we all agree on is that, except for Bruce's full head of hair, his pictures are exactly like little Clifton's at a comparable age.*

Raising our second little son in Asia was altogether different from Clifton 3rd's early years in the prefabs of the University of Chicago. With the aid of intelligent and caring household staff, I could have had a half dozen more babes. (Not really! I remain a devout family planner—even campaigner for a perfect population replacement ratio.) Bruce—adorable, cuddly, and robust as a two-month-old—was pampered by our immediate family and the cadre of others who complemented our domestic needs. He moved cheerfully within our spacious compound, with lots of interaction inside and outside the house. When Rawat, the gardener, washed Clif's car, he would fetch a second smaller brush for three-year-old Bruce, who insisted that the wheels were his responsibility.

All activities came to a halt whenever the bells announcing Bruce's favorite spicy-noodle hawker could be heard approaching. Bruce's head would pop up as he called out, "Treesa, Treesa, *che-chan fan, che-chan fan*." Theresa, our household *amah*, would hurriedly gather up two small bowls and, with a few coins in hand, run out to the edge of our driveway to buy the tasty snack from the peddler. The two of them could be seen squatting on their heels in traditional Asian style, devouring their savory morning treats.

Back in his earliest years, Bruce, customarily cheerful, also had a strong penchant for being intractable. His typical response to a complex problem, regardless of any suggested alternative: "I don'T wanT To Talk abouT iT," with emphatic emphasis on the *t*'s. I believe that Bruce's determination to be exact by his own standards was symptomatic of an innate drive for perfection.

Young Clifton, ever the showman, delighted in performing for Bruce's birthday parties, dressing up as a clown to beguile the preschoolers with self-taught magic tricks. On other occasions, Clifton and his expat classmates would role-play "The Three Little Pigs" and other fables, eliciting shrieks of amusement from their appreciative audience.

I shopped in the open markets almost every day with Bruce at my side. He sallied easily beside me in flip-flops on soapy wet floors, avoiding the freshly cut waste from chickens, fish, fruit, vegetables, and flowers being swept into open sewers. In his early years, before seat belts and safety car seats, Bruce would stand on the seat of my Triumph sports car, enabling him full view of the world through the window. But he quickly grew tall enough to sit in the passenger seat and survey the many fascinations

Clifton 3rd, the librarian
MA, University of Maryland,
Library and Information
Science

Anthony W. Collins, photographer

Bruce, the hotelier.
MBA, MSU College of Business

that my routine travels around Kuala Lumpur and environs allowed us to explore. Happily, Bruce and I both relished my meanderings.

A mere week after I had entered Bruce in a British half-day nursery school, my sturdy little boy arrived home with a fever contracted from a virus circulating among the children. Once the illness had run its course, I asked Bruce if he was ready to return, recalling the months I had sat with Clifton 3rd as he adjusted to the Hyde Park Baptist Nursery School in Chicago. Bruce pondered, mindful of the activities at home that he felt obliged to address, and thoughtfully concluded, "There are many important duties for me to attend to, so I guess I had better stay at home."

My thinking: Why rush? Bruce can return to the nursery school next term.

A couple of vignettes held significant meaning to Bruce's life upon our return to New York City, where both sons attended The Dalton School. Obviously, the new venue required some adjustment when contrasted with Bruce's life in Asia. His Dalton kindergarten teacher shared her concern about our son recoiling over the noise made by his rambunctious classmates. "As they play," she recounted, "Bruce will stand with his hands over his ears while the others romp about the rooftop (play area) with predictable high energy!"

Then secondly, in conversation with the school's principal, I realized we had perhaps provided too much serenity in our KL residence, resulting in Bruce's having been raised in an over-protected environment. In counterpoint, Bruce's Dalton playmates had benefitted from experiencing the clamor and crises of city life. Even the TV gangsters and cowboys had better-prepared the children for the outside world—particularly those challenged by electrifying New York City.

Clif and I took this information to heart and adjusted our parenting to compensate. We were delighted that by the end of the first of Bruce's five years at Dalton, he was as vigorous as the other young desperados.

In 1970 Bruce entered East Lansing's Hannah Middle School as the son of the university community's most noteworthy citizen, with all of the privileges and liabilities related to that role. While he faced new challenges, it was also where he discovered a door opening into his future life's path.

A back stairway near Bruce's bedroom in Cowles House led to a kitchen, pantry, food holding room—frequently jam-packed with undergrads all whirling in high activity—who surely influenced his choice of career. Professional chefs and a student waitstaff numbering as many as twenty-four, working under the auspices of MSU's Kellogg Hotel and Conference Center, facilitated our at-home entertaining. We hosted guests at least twice weekly, with triple that number during the semi-annual graduation receptions, when we received approximately five hundred graduates on each of three nights running. Though my menus for the Senior Receptions were simple—Catawba juice, stuffed celery, and cookies—the events still required scores of waiters to move among guests in the living room, patio, garden, and basement, where I screened a series of short films, from the sixty-second *Bambi Meets Godzilla* to the ten-minute *Imprint*, which I rented from the Museum of Modern Art.

These events became part of Bruce's everyday home life through his teen years. Occasionally during our parties, I would pop behind the scenes and find him chatting it up with the student servers. Who do you think made the stronger impact—the voice of Mom saying, "You have homework to finish" or a bunch of bright, young waiters schmoozing with our fun-loving child? How could he have not been bent toward the art of hospitality and a career in that industry? Those lively back-room capers led Bruce–following undergraduate and post-grad MBA studies–to his managerial posts with Westin, Sheraton, and Starwood hotels. Bruce also built and for six years operated his own business, a coffee house in Stamford, Connecticut. As an adjunct professor in several NYC metropolitan universities, he has taught hospitality and hotel/restaurant management.

Parenthood is a serious undertaking that requires not just love but sustained attention and interaction. The ideal upbringing for one child can totally miss the mark for another. Parenting penetrated my psyche. Months after Clifton's death, my moorings still shaken, Jim Spaniolo, one of MSU's outstanding deans and former assistant to Clif, added an unexpected lift to our spirits. Jim telephoned asking if we would return to campus for an event highlighting memorable moments of our lives in East Lansing. The occasion was to be labeled, "Trials and Triumph, 1970–1978." This retrospective from Jim and other caring friends was warmly transforming.

The program filled an entire day at the Wharton Center, beginning with Bill Wright (Wharton Center's executive director, 1992–2004), preceding Clif and me as we descended the handsome red-carpeted circular staircase of the Grand Tier into the caring embraces of some 150 friends, colleagues, and co-facilitators from our time on campus. A splendid lunch followed in the Center's Stoddard Lounge (one of the major gifts from valued families throughout our tenure), followed by a program of speakers in the Pasant Theater.

Jim opened a panel discussion with: "This convocation recognizes a critical, though sometimes overlooked, period of MSU history and accomplishment. It was a difficult, tumultuous time in many ways for MSU, yet despite the serious challenges, the university moved forward."

Next, President Peter McPherson said, "I think the theme, 'Years of Trial and Triumph' is an appropriate way to view this time in our national life and MSU's history. There were extraordinary demands for effective leadership then, and our university was fortunate to have the Whartons here. The convocation is a way to thank two wonderful people."

Four other panelists described significant achievements made during the Wharton years, sharing insights of emergencies addressed, storms quelled, and contemporary cultures inspired. With Jim presiding, the other speakers were Carl Taylor, professor of sociology and former Presidential Fellow; Roger Wilkinson, former VP for finance; James Bonnen, professor of agriculture economics; and Irving Taran, professor and later chairman of the art department. Each, in his own way had been an influential catalyst during our tenure. President (then Provost) Lou Anna Simon summarized the discussion with customary eloquence. The day concluded with a concert in the Cobb Great Hall by Billy Taylor, renowned jazz pianist, historian, and adored friend. For the occasion, he had composed an original work dedicated to Clifton 3rd. With their celestial beauty, the running chords of "In Loving Memory" left no hearts untouched.

As Billy Taylor's playing swept through the hall, the weight of our loss seemed to lift, allowing our spirits to soar with joyful reflections of young Clifton and our lives together so warmly recalled. Indeed, while the honor was bestowed in our name, the true meaning came from beloved friends who, knowing of our loss, had come together to tell us that they cared and that our lives had been a gift to each of them and to the legacy of MSU.

Clif and I often reflect upon the wealth of sensibilities that our sons' growing-up introduced to us. Nature was at its most generous in allowing us the joy of parental love. Through the boys, our own humanity leaped to new heights of awareness and understanding. We tried our utmost to be good parents—though Bruce once carped, "Yes, Mom, but sometimes you tried too hard." Clifton and Bruce were our ultimate lifetime gift from heaven reflected so wonderfully with Billy Taylor's absorbing tribute that evening to our elder son.

CHAPTER 13

At Home in Cooperstown

"Now I know why they moved here!" Pattye Snyder said to her husband, Bill, the first time these longtime friends from our Albany years visited our new home in Cooperstown.

Another guest stood silently surveying the scene from our living room windows, eventually opining, "Only God has a better view."

Our setting above Lake Otsego opened upon an extensive range of smoothly arched mountaintops to the east. The serenity instantly

slowed the rush of our busy lives. We were enchanted by the dazzling banks of yellow leaves speckled with ruby reds and jade greens all shimmering in soft breezes under sapphire blue skies seamed with wispy white clouds suggestive of Rene Magritte's playful renderings.

Clif and I had visited Don Curran's "house on the hill" in Cooperstown soon after my colleague from the Albany Law School Board of Trustees had completed building the spreading Californian ranch-style house. Years passed; we left Albany and moved to United Nations Plaza in New York City, where Clif took up the command of TIAA-CREF. Don died, and his property went on the market.

Then entered Norman Rice, esteemed past director of the Albany Institute of History and Art and a revered friend, who was an executor of Don's estate. Norman urged us to drive to Cooperstown to see the residence again. Once there, our decision to purchase the property was immediate and resolute. Along with the view, there was a second irresistible feature: a basement large enough to accommodate Clif's voluminous archives—all 750-cubic-feet worth. Soon after the closing, Norman gladdened our happy hearts even wider, saying, "I know that Don Curran would be thrilled that you

Our Doeclif Fall View of Lake Otsego. *Richard S. Duncan, photographer*

and Clif are now the owners of his dream house." We named our new home Doeclif.

Our reasons for purchasing a second home were practical—space enough for all our personal effects and a retreat from the cacophony of New York City. It was a perfect transitioning outpost. Moreover, our Golden Years would soon be upon us, raising the curtain on Doeclif as the ideal retreat from our multifaceted, peripatetic lives.

As we settled in, the property began to reflect more of our own tastes and travels. We undertook two major design additions: a three-tiered wraparound deck facing the lake, and a series of Japanese gardens. Shin Abe, a master Japanese gardener, and his team of workers arrived with two truckloads of huge rocks, which were set along the grass-lined drive-way. In the nooks and corners around the house Shin added small trees, which he sculpted and surrounded with black river stones, soft green moss, and streams of pea-stone to simulate water. Each composition added exotic surprises to delight the eye.

Accustomed to working with interior designers, who were essential to outfitting our residences at both MSU and SUNY, I called upon one of the connoisseurs in the decorators' trade, Jerry Copeland, who provided me access to New York City's Decoration and Design Building, where the general public is allowed entry only with a licensed professional. Together my masterful decorator and I selected fabrics and furnishings appropriate for our new country homestead.

In the course of time, we became warmly attached to a number of individuals essential to our evolving house, grounds and office. Melissa Manikas was a skilled professional assistant to Clif, taking charge of what actually was a multifaceted office. Over the years we developed an endearing and steadfast friendship with Melissa, her husband, Allan, and their two children. Mark Schoellig and his late wife, Jean, were another valued couple who, along with their two cherished sons, gave us marvelous attention and ingenious expertise. I was overjoyed to find several accomplished chefs who catered our "proper" lunches and dinners and whose fine cuisine was beautifully complimented by Colleen Spraker Raabe, an exemplary professional server. I soon came to rely on Colleen's management skills to direct waitstaff for large parties. Rounding out the loving-care-givers for Doeclif have been The Kanesmen, a team of grounds keepers, commandeered by David Pashley, who arrive weekly

Mark Schoellig, a skilled craftsman who constructed countless architectural features at Doeclif.

Melissa Manikas, our Doeclif office assistant, and Kathryn Sartori, executive administrator of our professional calendars and operations, pack and sort the Wharton archives for shipment to MSU.

throughout the summers (and winters, too, whenever the huge snow storms block access to the driveway). Outside the home is Kim Potts, the village's most coveted hair-stylist, known to pronounce, "I am a beautician NOT a magician." As one among many, I proclaim otherwise.

Of matchless importance has been our part-time driver, Wayne Granger, who transported me between Cooperstown and Albany's private airport terminal when there were board meetings to attend in Bartlesville, Battle Creek, and Washington, DC, as well as personal drives between our home in Cooperstown and the apartment in New York City. Wayne has proven to be a winsome and popular local personality steadfast in his attention to Clif and me.

As newcomers to the community, we delighted in exploring Cooperstown. The population, as given in the 2010 census, was 1,852. We found classic colonial architecture still conspicuous, with slender white church steeples that peek above rows of wood-framed houses. The side streets are lined with neatly painted bungalows fronted with broad porches and closely trimmed lawns. Main Street boasts a single traffic light, as if to confirm status as a small upstate village. One could never miss the huge flapping banner suspended across Main Street announcing each week's community events. A unifying feature identifies places of preeminence: the tall, white columns that soldier the entrances to the

Fenimore Art Museum, the Bassett Hospital, the Village Library, and the four-star/four-diamond-rated Otesaga Hotel.

One of my favorite discoveries was the Clark Sports Center, which offers unparalleled physical training programs for all ages—including workout sessions with Jim Jordan, our super-smart personal trainer, known for pushing, pushing, pushing us always just a little bit harder (after which we go home to collapse). Close by is a helicopter pad, where out-of-town guests set down for afternoon visits, with lunch and a matinee at Glimmerglass Opera.

The bedrock site of our explorations was the Mary Imogene Bassett Hospital, a facility that provides advanced professional services to the region, and where Clif and I both have received extraordinary life-saving care over a number of years.

Of course, the great headline attraction of Cooperstown is that sports holy-of-holies, the Baseball Hall of Fame, which is a major contributor to the town's economic base. The Hall's popularity also invites numbers of independent shops promoting the sale of baseball paraphernalia and memorabilia, restaurants, B&Bs, and a variety of services to meet the needs of thousands of tourists who arrive en masse during the summer months.

Major commercial food chains have not been welcomed within the village, though they would love to have access to the hordes of baseball fans who overrun the area every summer. Local legend maintains that the village's most prominent citizen and benefactor, Jane Clark, a firmly protective patron of Cooperstown's original, small-town image, would promptly take action whenever a giant chain expressed interest in any of the vacant storefronts. Jane simply would buy up the property, effectively denying the corporate hopefuls an opening wedge. Independent family-owned businesses have for decades fed the hungry tourists. Cooperstown is maintained as a picture-perfect early American village, updated with state-of-the-art amenities and capable technicians to manage the necessities of the twenty-first century.

Cooperstown's provincial environment stood in sharp contrast to what we were accustomed. Common to our professional lives was routine travel in and out of private airports, limousines rushing us to corporate offices, factory tours sampling products, reams of reports to read and official documents to sign. Once during a TV interview, a reporter commenting on our demanding schedules asked, "Do you and your husband ever have time to be alone together?" I tartly responded, "Well we have two sons!" (She blushed, saying, "I wasn't expecting that!")

Clif and I had faced seventeen years in academe and thirty years in corporate. Though often breathless, we actually thrived. However, the suggestion of a more leisurely pace to be found beside Lake Otsego was very seductive to us both.

From the beginning of our thirty-plus years in residence, we have been generously received and recognized by the multigenerational residents. Even today, descendants of the Cooper family and other local ancestries retain their heritage as landed gentry, even though many are only summer occupants of longtime family-owned properties. It was very pleasant to be welcomed by these cultured people, who accepted Clif and me warmly to the region's social A-list.

Being courted by the leadership of the local philanthropic boards was most flattering. Though I ascribed my initial popularity to perceived fund-raising potential, board compositions are reflections of an organization's image. Thus, the appeals to us were indicative of how we were perceived within the community. Initially I declined all inquiries, as my most dedicated commitment lay with FCI and the corporate boards. But eventually, as my external responsibilities declined, I agreed to accept the Glimmerglass Opera trusteeship in response to the winsome persuasion of Katherine Cooper Cary, great-great-granddaughter of James Fenimore Cooper, village founder and author of *The Last of the Mohicans* and countless Leatherstocking stories. Katherine and her journalist brother, Henry, were beloved Cooperstown loyalists. But more than that, they were both super-gracious patrons of Glimmerglass Opera.

Independently established by the arts-minded locals, Glimmerglass competed prominently on the national and international stages of summer theater. Under the leadership of Paul Kellogg and, later, Francesca Zambello, the company attracted world-class maestros, directors, set designers, and guest performers, becoming a cultural jewel for upstate New York.

Inspired by the warm invitation and the highest of high standards set by the artistic leadership of the company, I was happy to join up. Beyond the customary monetary contribution expected from all board members, I looked for other ways to make a useful contribution. When National Public Radio offered to broadcast the exquisite Glimmerglass production

Views of and about Doeclif

of *Il Re Pastore*[1], there was one catch: Glimmerglass would be expected to pay a portion of the production fees. Without being asked, but knowledgeable about the details of the dilemma, I approached Phillips Petroleum to underwrite the broadcast. To everyone's delight, my request was approved, resulting in Phillips Petroleum giving Glimmerglass its first corporate grant.

Another favorable initiative was bringing Albany patrons to the Cooperstown productions. I began by contacting Norman Rice and Anne Older, president of Albany's Preservation League, who gathered a large number of fellow opera devotees to make a round trip to Glimmerglass for a matinee performance, after which Clif and I hosted a post-opera dinner party at Doeclif. This initial event launched the company's Albany outpost, which remained active for a number of years. Concurrent with these and another of my Glimmerglass activities was working together with Bill Oliver, Glimmerglass's senior-most development officer. Oliver, now retired, was a nobleman within the profession. Our friendship with him and his partner, Michael Willis, is a longtime coveted treasure of Clif and mine. Joan Desens has taken up the directorship of development with her own splendid aptitude and grace, allowing us to continue my relationship to the opera as if I were still a board member.

The beguiling Glimmerglass performances provided exhilarating entertainment for our visiting guests: educators, musicians, political types, scholars—many were Caucasian, some Asian, and a number of dearly loved Black patricians. It was an extraordinary time of togetherness.

We were sometimes suspicious of a slight undercurrent of racial animus harbored by a few of the locals. Once at a fancy social event, the wife of a prominent community leader approached with, "Dolores, mind if I ask you a personal question?"

Expecting conversation about my recent cardiac emergencies, I invited the question.

"How much do you know about your slave history?" she asked.

My response: "Nothing!" I was dumbfounded!

What I did know was that my ancestry was well documented, revealing that my great-great-grandfather, Thomas Bradford Sr., born in 1842, was a Free Negro. Was that what she was so curious about? Had her

1 Beekman Cannon letter to Dolores Wharton, July 20, 1991.

Cheeka
Bruce's schnauzer,
our surrogate
grandchild

question preceded a genealogical conversation or were she an inquiring historian, I could have accepted the query as relevant to serious discussion. After considerable reflection, I concluded that by posing the question, this woman was referring me back to the inferior status assigned to descendants of former slaves in America.

However mean-spirited her intent, the incident was unworthy of affecting me emotionally or of my wasting any effort in trying to enlighten her. I dismissed the conversation as irrelevant, though I did seek Clif in the crowd, promptly taking his always caring hand.

Heiress Jane Clark enhanced our community affiliations when she invited Clif to serve as trustee on three boards: her family's Clark Foundation, the Bassett Medical Center, and the New York State Historical Association. Jane is very much a "to the manner born" high priestess of the land—literally thousands of acres of it. Though her name is always spoken in respectful tones, she is frequently referred to by her first name. I bet if one mailed an envelope simply addressed to "Jane," the Cooperstown postman would deliver it promptly to her door the next morning.

We found summers in our adopted village to be a pleasant flurry of cocktail receptions and dinner parties—stylistically, a low-key East Hampton. Clif and I have thoroughly enjoyed the generosity of our valued, too-many-to-name hosts in receiving us in their homes, gardens, country club parties, birthday and anniversary celebrations, and in everyone's favorite venue for private events, the Otesaga Hotel. And it has been our great pleasure to return those many splendid invitations in gatherings at Doeclif. However, there was one particular response given us from among our friends in the community that I can never adequately reciprocate. The genuine empathy expressed by many individuals from all strata throughout the community upon young Clifton's death demonstrated to my husband and me a generosity of spirit that will remain ever in our hearts.

For Clif and me, Doeclif and Cooperstown have been the perfect retreat for us to step away from our professional and energy-sapping peripatetic lives. Always, in preparing to depart Doeclif for a long absence, we check all the windows, tightly draw the drapes, double-lock the doors, and activate the security system. As our overloaded car backs out of the garage into the driveway, I bid our home a silent farewell with a short prayer to remain safe and at peace until our return. This little ritual is an affectionate nod for the well-being of our home. Why this private moment between me and our house-on-the-hill? I am not really sure. Perhaps, as a born New Yorker, I remain a newcomer to dear Cooperstown, for which my pledge to return shall always be my promise and my prayer.

A Question of Race and Gender

My DNA shows that I possess both Black genes and white genes. In a world where race blinds, perplexes, distorts—and where the racist doctrine "one drop of Black blood" continues to affirm one's ethnicity as Black and Black only—I firmly and proudly identify as an American Black woman. My husband, who like me has Black and white genes, also identifies as an American Black.

There is a subtle—yet not *so* subtle—issue underlying these pages: racial and gender stereotyping.

The problems became sharply evident during my early days in promoting FCI. There were many in my audiences who perceived my mission—dedicated to minorities and women—as "developmental" or "remedial" tutorials, designed for the underqualified seeking a niche on the margins of the workplace. It was also especially aggravating to learn that even some Blacks and women prejudged my efforts as a kind of defection, a way of siding with "them" instead of "us."

My years serving on the boards of major corporations, often as the first Black and first woman, brought into focus just how great a challenge it would be for women and minorities to break through that insidious glass ceiling. Ideally no woman would again be told, "You should be at home caring for your husband," nor minorities be expected to "know your place."

The inhumane transgressions imposed upon American Black people have persisted despite the passage of centuries and laws, and despite all our struggles, strides, and achievements. In essence, a brand has been permanently and brutally burned upon people of color that, until the

OPPOSITE: Portrait of Dolores Wharton, 1962
ARTIST: Krishen Khanna, oil on canvas
Richard Walker, photographer

end of days, they are to be denied human dignity and respect. This stain marking us American Blacks is an indelible curse never to be forgotten nor forgiven, though it was the moral sin of our white enslavers and ancestors who forged the vicious hatred four centuries ago.

Another racial burden endured by people of color is the failure by many to recognize the tremendous diversity among Black people. We are not all poor or uneducated. Some perceive all of us as born into the same circumstances, with neither intelligence nor talent, unless sports-related, or with food preferences limited to watermelon and fried chicken. Nevertheless, we can boast countless Black contributors to our society: scientists, university presidents, inventors, poets, artists, architects, opera divas, military generals, authors, Nobel laureates, senators, and, yes, an American president! We, in fact, reflect all hues, sizes, generations, and fields.

I fully endorse the imperative that Blacks should not forget where we have come from, but it is no less important to remember where we are and where we want to go. While acknowledging the burdens we have carried and still bear, we should also celebrate our accomplishments. Evidence of this progress came to me personally in November 2016, when Clifton and I were honored as Black corporate pioneers by the Executive Leadership Council. We were thrilled to be recognized by the ELC. Its guest list comprised 2,400 members, some 90 percent of whom were Black leaders from upper management and officers from within America's corporate executive suites. This group bore dramatic witness to the progress that has been achieved in corporate America. But regardless of the reality of Black people operating in mainstream society, the furtively denied caste system in this country openly attempts to negate much of what Black people have contributed to our nation.

Serendipity has exposed me to less of the scornful, racist humiliation suffered by so many others. It has been my good fortune to benefit from my family's five generations–long social standing, my early education, my professional appointments, my experience abroad, and marriage to a man of intelligence and accomplishment. But my central grounding was the shared, sixty-nine-year love story between Clif and me, enhanced by the sacred gift of our two beloved sons.

We are each and every one of us racial beings who participate in multiple dimensions of worldly affairs and cultures. In writing our personal journals, race issues cannot be denied or ignored. But we are much more than our individual lineage—more complex, more nuanced, more varied, more individual, more humane. In my reflections, these issues have been visited, though quite possibly not yet completed. Surely there are many more accountings yet to be exposed.

As the king advises Alice in Lewis Carroll's *Alice in Wonderland,* "Begin at the beginning and go on till you come to the end: then stop."

But, please know that I intend to explore, more and more, as long as there is yet more to explore.

ACKNOWLEDGMENTS

There are my readers, all incomparable friends, all rich with literary intelligence, all valued for their sensitivity to humankind:

Kenneth Beachler	**Judith Moyers**
Madeleine Condit	**Rita Nalebuff**
Paula DiPerna	**Bill Oliver**
Joseph Giovannini	**Bob Perrin**
James Harkness	**Harriet Segal**
Madelyn Jennings	**Geoffrey Steck**
Donna Stein Korn	**Michael Willis**
Bill Moyers	**Albert Wilson**

I want to thank each and every one of my eagle-eyed commentators for taking the time to read my manuscript and to share comments that have moved my thinking forward.

Paul Block, novelist, journalist, former editor-in-chief of Book Creations Inc., and former executive producer of the Albany *Times Union*, accepted with grace and diligence the task to review and edit the entire text. I am in Paul's debt for the exacting professional skills he brought to my writing.

Former *New York Times*-man **Jeremy Gerard** brought his skills as editor and cultural critic to my work on the final manuscript.

Juan Perez has always responded with great kindness and relentless patience my myriad cries of distress to adjust endless computer complexities. Without his technical genius to call upon this manuscript would still be simply an idea.

Erin Kirk New, award-winning book designer, infused her multiple talents as artist and layout typographer with a uniquely personal commitment to excellence. I am deeply grateful for her patience and constancy throughout this project.

Cynthia A. Ghering, Director University Archives and Historical Collections, and her MSU staff were an invaluable resource.

Kathryn Sartori has faithfully and ever-skillfully provided constant support for the overall production of this book. Her superb professionalism has served as a solid rock from which Clifton and I have benefited for some thirty years.

As for the heart of the matter: There would have been no beginning, no persistent encouragement, no relentless fact finder, no hope of finishing this manuscript without the loving determination of my adored husband. Thus, I dedicate its reality to the meaning of my life, **CLIFTON WHARTON, JR.**

Video Links

1. "Cowles House: Art in Residence, 1971"

    http://onthebanks.msu.edu/Object/1-4-17C7/cowles-house-art
    -in-residence-1971/

2. "Dedication of the Wharton Center for Performing Arts,"
    September 26, 1982

    http://onthebanks.msu.edu/Object/1-4-1804/dedication
    -ceremonies-for-the-wharton-center-for-the-performing
    -arts-1982/

3. "Trial and Triumph: The Wharton Years, 1970-1978. A Tribute Event
    to Clifton R. Wharton, Jr. And Dolores Wharton," October 27, 2000

    http://onthebanks.msu.edu/Object/1-4-1435/trial—triumph-the
    -wharton-years-19701978-a-tribute-to-clifton-r-wharton-jr
    —dolores-wharton/Wharton_

INDEX